# STIR

# STIR
# CHRISTINE
# MANFIELD

FOREWORD BY CHARLIE TROTTER

PHOTOGRAPHY BY ASHLEY BARBER

ICI LA PRESS

Ici La Press
694 Main St. South
Woodbury, CT 06798
www.icilapress.com

ISBN 1-931605-14-9

Printed and bound in Thailand

First published by Penguin Books Australia Ltd 2001

10 9 8 7 6 5 4 3 2 1

Designed by Guy Mirabella
Photography by Ashley Barber

**STIR** the pot **STIR** the senses **STIR** yourself **STIR** it up

**STIR** your imagination **STIR** into action **STIR** your memory

**STIR** fry **STIR** the blood **STIR** it round **STIR** your tastebuds

good food is essential to well-being **KEEP STIRRING**

Contents

# Foreword by Charlie Trotter

Christine Manfield has been a pioneer for a remarkably long time. In the mid-'80s when she opened her ground-breaking restaurant, Paramount, she made quite an impression. In fact, foodies and gourmands from around the world took notice and came to sample her personal and original fare. She was among the very first to incorporate subtle (and not so subtle!) Asian influences into European-based cuisine. The results were stunning, and still inspire to this day. Now Chris is exploring the influences of India and a variety of other regions. In her hands, these disparate influences are not only coherent, they all make sense.

It seems to me, Chris is the restless sort – intellectually, that is. She is always questioning, probing, incorporating, traveling, theorizing, embracing, explaining, reading, eating, exploring, studying, quizzing, playing, and, most of all, remembering! The results, when she returns to her kitchen or her laptop, are truly exciting. Hers is a fabulously original take on the beauties and possibilities of modern food. Although Chris is a prolific author and has documented much of her work already, she has utterly hit pay dirt with *STIR*, her latest magnificent effort. Of particular appeal to me is going through this luscious work and finding a glut of mouth-watering recipes that are not merely delicious, but also quite healthy. I can start by referring you to the *Chickpea and Harissa Soup.* This preparation explodes with a mixture of elegant flavors – garlic, cumin, mint, and tomato – and then is gorgeously touched with the profound, clean heat of harissa. The chickpeas themselves add body and a satiny texture. In all, it is substance and exotic enticement perfectly intertwined.  Or, try the *Spiced Eggplant Pickle and Yogurt Salad.* It is actually incredibly simple to prepare, but the resulting flavors are overwhelmingly complex. Tart, sweet, sour, and hot are all rolled into one, and then speared with the penetrating notes of fish sauce and cilantro. True brilliance is at work here!  Maybe you just want to go straight to the brink. In that case try the *Coconut Chili Scallops with Pomelo Salad.* The flavors and textures in the dish meld so remarkably, they're haunting.

*STIR* inspires for a number of reasons, but chief among them is that these are recipes that are meant for both the home cook and the professional, a rare find in today's cookery books. As Chris Manfield continues to push the envelope and explore the possibilities of influence from around the world, we are all the beneficiaries.  With this inspiring collection of recipes and images, Chris has given us a true gift – in return, we can only offer a resounding "Three Cheers!"

# Introduction

Spice pastes – hot and pungent or mellow or fragrant – are the cornerstones of many of the cuisines of the world, and certainly of the food I like to prepare and eat. Dishes made using spice pastes benefit from the preservative, digestive and antiseptic properties of spices, meaning that they are not only delicious but healthy, too. However, making your own spice pastes for use in a recipe can be complicated and time-consuming. Realizing that using ready-made spice pastes would save people valuable time and, for many, remove the fear of the unknown and the intimidation of a lengthy cooking process, I embarked on the production of a commercial range of spice preparations.

After we closed the Paramount Store in 1995, we found it impossible to keep up with the demand for our products, particularly the very popular spice pastes. We were making them in the kitchen in our spare hours outside full restaurant service, and soon realized that the next big step had to be taken – getting a quality manufacturer to reproduce them, on a much larger scale, in the same way that I would make them, keeping true to their flavor without the use of preservatives or additives. And so in 2000 the Christine Manfield Spice Collection was born. I designed the products to open the door to the seductive world of spice, create harmony and equilibrium in your diet, fire your imagination, and instill passion and pride in your cooking. This book is designed as a companion and guide to the range. You can either make the spice pastes from scratch following the basic recipes at the start of each chapter, or purchase them ready-made when you find yourself short of time. Using the ready-made products is a totally acceptable short cut!

The recipes in the book build on my comprehensive volume *Spice* and celebrate the diversity of contemporary everyday Australian cooking. Each recipe given here will provide maximum flavor and seasoning for your food. The preparations include fast, hot cooking such as stir-frying or barbecuing, and long, slow methods, such as braising, that don't require constant attention – you can leave the dish to work miracles unchecked while you busy yourself elsewhere. The recipes showcase the versatility of each product and have been devised with the intention of using minimum effort for maximum effect and taste. Rather than complex, restaurant-style cooking that necessitates several preparations and steps to reach the final outcome, these recipes are designed for simple cooking at home. I hope they will inspire you to get busy in your kitchen.

I remain a staunch advocate of the philosophy that life is too short to eat bad food. Please join me in that quest by taking an active interest in good, healthy, interesting cooking with spice pastes.

NOTE: If you are using the ready-made products from my range, each jar contains roughly 12 portions for any given preparation.

# Chili Jam

My chili jam is more complex and refined than many of its commercial counterparts (sambals, etc.) and you'll find it has a multitude of uses in many of the recipes in this book beyond this chapter. I'm sure you'll find it useful in some of your favorite recipes, too. Slow, prolonged cooking time gives it an enduring and lingering sweetness, but although it is referred to as a jam, it is not to be confused with confectionery jams or jellies – spread it on toast for breakfast at your peril! The basic recipe on page 6 does not translate easily into a smaller quantity, but don't worry – it quickly disappears because it's so addictive.

3 lb. (1.5 kg) large red Anaheim *or* Dutch chilies,
  chopped
10 oz. (300 g) Thai chilies, chopped
8 large onions, chopped
15 large cloves garlic, chopped
4 cups (1 l) vegetable oil
1¼ cups (300 ml) Tamarind Liquid (page 200)
⅝ cup (125 g) brown sugar (*or* palm sugar, shaved)
extra vegetable oil, for sealing

## Chili jam

**1** Blend chili, onion, garlic, and oil to a smooth paste in a food processor. **2** Cook paste in a wide, heavy-bottomed pan over low heat until dark red – this will take up to 12 hours of continuous slow cooking and occasional stirring. **3** Stir in tamarind liquid and brown sugar and cook very slowly for 2 hours more. **4** Spoon into sterilized jars, cover with a film of oil, and seal when cool. Keeps, refrigerated, for up to 3 months.

*Makes 2 quarts (2 liters)*

2 medium onions, finely chopped
3 large cloves garlic, finely chopped
1 tbsp. finely chopped ginger
4 Thai chilies, finely chopped
1½ tbsp. (20 ml) vegetable oil
1 cup (250 g) crunchy peanut butter
4 tbsp. CHILI JAM (page 6)
1½ cups (400 ml) coconut milk
½ cup (125 ml) light soy sauce
¾ cup (150 g) brown sugar
6 tbsp. (80 ml) strained lime juice
⅓ cup (100 ml) rice vinegar
3½ tbsp. (50 ml) fish sauce

## Peanut chili sauce

**1** Sweat onion, garlic, ginger, and chili in oil over moderate heat until softened. **2** Add peanut butter, CHILI JAM, and coconut milk and bring to the boil, stirring frequently to prevent sticking. Cook, uncovered, over gentle heat for 15 minutes, or until thickened. **3** Add remaining ingredients, bring back to the boil, and cook for 5 minutes. **4** Taste and, if necessary, adjust seasoning. Serve with satay prawns or chicken, grilled meats or gado-gado (Indonesian vegetable salad). Will keep, refrigerated in a sealed container, for up to 2 weeks. Reheat gently to serve.

*Makes 1 quart (1 liter)*

## Chili salt tofu with bean sprout salad

4 stems Chinese broccoli, sliced

7 oz. (200 g) bean sprouts

12 snow peas, finely sliced

8 oz. (250 g) snow pea sprouts

2 oz. (50 g) tatsoi leaves *or* watercress sprigs

vegetable oil, for deep-frying

8 fresh tofu squares

4 tsp. CHILI JAM (page 6)

1 large red Anaheim *or* Dutch chili, seeded and
   cut into julienne

6 scallions, sliced diagonally

**Chili salt crust**

2 large dried Anaheim *or* Dutch chilies

4 black peppercorns

1 tsp. sea salt

2 tbsp. rice flour

**Chili dressing**

¼ cup (60 ml) fish sauce

1 clove garlic, finely chopped

1 Thai chili, finely chopped

3 tsp. strained lime juice

2 tsp. sugar

**1** To make the chili salt crust, dry-roast chilies, peppercorns, and sea salt over gentle heat until slightly colored. Cool, then grind to a fine powder and mix with rice flour. **2** To make the salad, steam broccoli for a few minutes until tender (the stems will take longer than the leaves, so remove the leaves as they cook or add halfway through to ensure even cooking). Combine broccoli with bean sprouts, snow peas, snow pea sprouts, and tatsoi. **3** Mix chili dressing ingredients thoroughly and pour over salad. Toss well and allow to stand for 15 minutes before serving. **4** To cook tofu, heat oil in a deep-fryer or large pot to 350°F (180°C). Coat tofu squares with chili salt crust and fry, a few at a time, for 2 minutes, or until pale golden and crisp on the surface. They will float to the top when cooked. Remove carefully with a mesh skimmer and drain on paper towels. **5** Arrange salad on plates, sit the fried tofu on top with the CHILI JAM, pepper strips, and green onion, and serve.

*Serves 4*

## Crispy sweet-and-sour fish with cucumber salad

vegetable oil, for deep-frying

2 tsp. Sichuan Spice Salt (page 200)

1 tbsp. rice flour

8 whole small red mullet *or* rainbow smelt, cleaned and scaled (see Note)

**Chili sauce**

4 tsp. (20 ml) vegetable oil

4 scallions, finely sliced

2 cloves garlic, finely chopped

1 tsp. finely chopped ginger

4 tsp. CHILI JAM (page 6)

3 tbsp. (40 ml) Chinese black vinegar

4 tsp. (20 ml) light soy sauce

2 tsp. fish sauce

2 tbsp. sugar

⅓ cup (100 ml) White Chicken Stock (page 202)

**Cucumber salad**

1 cucumber, peeled and seeded

4 scallions, finely sliced

1 large red Anaheim *or* Dutch chili, finely sliced

2 tbsp. peanuts, roasted and chopped

¼ cup shredded mint leaves

**1** To make chili sauce, heat oil in a wok and fry scallions, garlic, and ginger for 30 seconds, or until fragrant. Add CHILI JAM, vinegar, soy sauce, fish sauce, and sugar and simmer for 3 minutes. Add stock and simmer for another 5 minutes. Set aside and reheat when ready to serve. **2** To make cucumber salad, cut cucumber into small pieces and mix in a bowl with green onion, chili, peanuts, and mint. **3** To cook fish, heat oil in a deep-fryer or large pot to 350°F (180°C). Mix spice salt with flour and coat each fish with seasoned flour. Deep-fry fish for 4 to 6 minutes, depending on size and thickness. Remove from oil with mesh skimmer and drain on paper towels. **4** To serve, divide cucumber salad between 4 plates, sit crispy fish on top, and spoon chili sauce over.

*Serves 4*

Note: Other suitable fish include red snapper, catfish, and cod.

1 cup (200 g) jasmine rice, washed
cold water
2 tsp. sea salt, roasted and ground
2 Thai chilies, roasted and ground
2 tbsp. rice flour
4¼ lb. (125 g) snapper fillets (see Note)
⅓ cup (100 ml) olive oil
½ cup cilantro leaves
8 tsp. CHILI JAM (page 6)
1 tbsp. Fried Garlic Slices (page 201)

# Pan-fried snapper fillets with steamed rice and chili jam

**1** Put rice in a saucepan and add enough cold water to measure 1½ in. (4 cm) over rice. Cover with a lid and cook on moderate heat for about 15 minutes, or until water has been absorbed and rice is soft and fluffy. **2** Mix salt, chili and rice flour together. Coat snapper fillets with seasoned flour. **3** Heat oil in a frying pan until hot and shallow-fry fish over moderate heat until cooked, turning halfway through. Cooking time should be about 6 minutes (3 minutes on each side). Flesh should be white and firm without being dry or breaking open. **4** Remove fish from pan and rest on paper towels. **5** Spoon hot rice onto plates, sit fish on top, and garnish with cilantro leaves, CHILI JAM, and fried garlic slices.

*Serves 4*

Note: Other suitable fish include mackerel, cod, sea bass, gurnard, bream, sea mullet, or any tropical reef fish.

8 large (1-week-old) eggs
1 tsp. sea salt
3 tbsp. (40 ml) light soy sauce
1½ tbsp. (20 ml) dark soy sauce
3 star anise
2 tbsp. Chinese oolong (black tea) leaves
1 tbsp. jasmine tea leaves
8 tsp. CHILI JAM (page 6)
selection of condiments, to serve (optional)

## Spiced tea eggs with chili jam

**1** Cook eggs in simmering water for 8 minutes, or until hard-boiled. Remove from heat and plunge into cold water. Crack shells gently with a spoon until finely cracked all over. Put eggs in a saucepan with remaining ingredients, except CHILI JAM and condiments. **2** Cover with water and bring to the boil. Cover pot, reduce heat to low, and simmer for 30 minutes. Remove pot from heat and allow eggs to cool in tea infusion for 3 to 4 hours for flavor to develop fully. **3** Remove eggs from liquid and carefully peel off cracked shells. The eggs should have a marbled appearance. **4** Cut eggs in half and serve with CHILI JAM as a condiment along with pickled vegetables (jiang cai), preserved mustard greens (gai choy), or bok choy. These preserves are readily available from Chinese grocers.

*Serves 4*

## Crab, pork, and chili dumplings

24 wonton wrappers
1 egg white
rice flour
**Crab and pork stuffing**
2½ oz. (75 g) lean ground pork
2 tsp. Chinese Shaoxing rice wine
½ tsp. freshly ground white pepper
6½ oz. (200 g) cooked crabmeat
2 bok choy leaves, blanched
   and shredded
8 water chestnuts, finely diced
4 stalks Chinese celery (kun choy) *or* plain celery,
   finely chopped
2 scallions, finely sliced
2 tbsp. chopped cilantro leaves
2 tsp. finely chopped ginger
2 tsp. fish sauce
2 tsp. light soy sauce
2 tsp. CHILI JAM (page 6)
**Dipping sauce**
3½ tbsp. (50 ml) Chinese black vinegar
1 tsp. fine ginger slivers

**1** To make stuffing, knead pork with rice wine and white pepper in a bowl. Add remaining ingredients, mixing thoroughly by hand to combine. Roll into 24 small balls and flatten slightly with your fingers. **2** Lay out 4 wonton wrappers at a time on work surface. Place stuffing on center of each wrapper, brush edges lightly with egg white, and fold over, pressing edges together to seal. Wrap around finger and press ends together. **3** Lay prepared dumplings in a single layer on a tray sprinkled with rice flour to prevent sticking. Continue to make dumplings until stuffing mix is all used. **4** Cook several dumplings at a time, in boiling water for 3 minutes. Remove carefully with a slotted spoon. **5** Make dipping sauce by combining black vinegar and ginger slivers. Serve dumplings with sauce.

*Serves 4*

4 large eggs

3 tbsp. (40 ml) vegetable oil

4 tsp. CHILI JAM (page 6)

2 tsp. BLACK PEPPER AND LEMONGRASS STIR-FRY PASTE
  (page 82)

2 tsp. chili bean paste (toban jiang)

¾ cup (200 ml) Shrimp Stock (page 202) *or* White
  Chicken Stock (page 202)

13 oz. (410 g) fresh Chinese egg noodles (see Note)

4 oz. (125 g) Chinese red roasted pork, sliced

12 green king shrimp, shelled and deveined

2 squid tubes, cleaned and cut lengthwise into thin strips

7 oz. (200 g) bean sprouts

2 large red Anaheim *or* Dutch chilies, finely sliced

4 tbsp. cilantro leaves

# Combination stir-fried Chinese egg noodles

**1** Beat 3 of the eggs in a bowl. Heat half the oil in a wok and add beaten egg, tilting pan to make a thin omelette. Cook until set. Turn out of wok, roll up, and slice finely. Set aside. **2** Heat remaining oil in wok and fry CHILI JAM, BLACK PEPPER AND LEMONGRASS STIR-FRY PASTE and chili bean paste together for 1 minute, or until fragrant. **3** Mix in stock and, when simmering, add noodles and toss to combine. Cook for 3 minutes, or until noodles have softened. Add remaining egg, stirring quickly with a chopstick so egg forms threads through the sauce. **4** Add pork, shrimp, and squid and continue to toss over high heat until just cooked, about 2 minutes. Add bean sprouts and omelette strips. **5** Sprinkle with chili slices and cilantro and serve.

*Serves 4*

Note: If fresh noodles are unavailable, dried noodles should be blanched for use in this recipe.

## Chicken and stir-fried chili vegetables

4 chicken thighs
3 tbsp. (40 ml) light soy sauce
2 tsp. sesame oil
vegetable oil, for deep-frying
1 tsp. Sichuan Spice Salt (page 200)
1 tbsp. finely chopped garlic
2 tsp. finely chopped ginger
2 Thai chilies, finely chopped
1 tsp. freshly ground black pepper
3 tbsp. (40 ml) fish sauce
1½ tbsp. (20 ml) Chinese oyster sauce
6 napa cabbage hearts, blanched
   and halved lengthwise
12 snow peas, trimmed
7 oz. (200 g) bean sprouts
½ red bell pepper, finely sliced
8 tsp. CHILI JAM (page 6)
1 cup Thai basil leaves

**1** Cut each chicken thigh into 2 pieces at the joint. Mix soy sauce with sesame oil and rub into flesh of chicken. **2** Heat vegetable oil in a deep-fryer or large pot to 350°F (180°C) and fry chicken pieces, a few at a time, for 8 minutes, or until crisp and golden. Check if flesh is cooked by inserting a skewer – flesh should be pink and juices should run clear. Remove chicken from oil with a slotted spoon and rest on paper towel. Sprinkle with Sichuan spice salt. **3** Heat a wok, add about 1 tbsp. vegetable oil, and fry garlic, ginger, chilies, and black pepper for a few seconds until fragrant. **4** Add fish and oyster sauces, then toss in napa cabbage, snow peas, bean sprouts, red pepper strips, and CHILI JAM. Cook over high heat, tossing to combine, for 1 to 2 minutes, or until vegetables have wilted. **5** Add basil leaves, toss, and remove from heat immediately. **6** Arrange stir-fried vegetables in a pile on plates and top with fried chicken pieces. Serve extra CHILI JAM as a condiment, if desired.

*Serves 4*

## Eggplant sambal with chili pork

8 Japanese eggplants, trimmed
6 bok choy leaves
2 tsp. Chinese Shaoxing rice wine
2 tsp. fish sauce
½ tsp. freshly ground white pepper
2½ oz. (80 g) lean ground pork
4 tsp. (20 ml) vegetable oil
4 scallions, finely sliced
1 tsp. finely chopped ginger
1 tsp. finely chopped garlic
1 Thai chili, finely chopped
4 tsp. CHILI JAM (page 6)
4 tsp. (20 ml) light soy sauce
4 tsp. (20 ml) Chinese black vinegar
2 tsp. sugar
1 tsp. sesame oil
¼ cup cilantro leaves

**1** Cut eggplants into quarters lengthwise, to make thick batons. **2** Line a large steamer basket with bok choy leaves and lay eggplant slices on the cabbage in a single layer. Cover with lid and steam over boiling water for 15 minutes, or until eggplant has wilted and is tender. Discard bok choy leaves when eggplant is cooked. Remove and discard skin from eggplant. **3** While eggplant is steaming, work rice wine, fish sauce, and pepper through the ground pork with your fingers, kneading thoroughly. **4** Heat oil in a wok and fry scallions, ginger, garlic, and chili for 30 seconds, or until fragrant. **5** Add CHILI JAM, soy sauce, vinegar, and sugar. When simmering, add pork. Toss over high heat to ensure even cooking. Cook for 5 minutes, or until pork has browned. Taste and, if necessary, adjust seasoning. **6** To serve, arrange steamed eggplant slices on a large plate and spoon chili pork over. Drizzle with sesame oil and sprinkle with cilantro leaves.
*Serves 4*

one 5 lb. (2.3 kg) Chinese roasted duck

12½ oz. (400 g) fresh rice noodle sheets, cut into
    ¾ in. (2 cm) wide strips

2 tsp. sesame oil

4 tsp. (20 ml) vegetable oil

2 tsp. chili oil

2 cloves garlic, finely chopped

2 small Thai chilies, finely chopped

1 tsp. finely chopped ginger

4 tsp. CHILI JAM (page 6)

1 Chinese pork (lap cheong) sausage, finely sliced

6½ oz. (200 g) bean sprouts

6 scallions, finely sliced

3 tbsp. (40 ml) sweet soy sauce (kecap manis)

2 tsp. fish sauce

2 eggs, beaten

1 bunch Chinese chives, snipped

1 tbsp. Fried Garlic Slices (page 201)

## Roasted duck noodles with chili

**1** Slice meat and crispy skin from duck and cut into 1 in. (2.5 cm) pieces. Discard bones and fat. **2** Put noodles in a pot and pour boiling water over to soften. Drain noodles in a colander and toss with sesame oil to prevent sticking. **3** Heat wok, add vegetable and chili oils, and fry garlic, chilies, and ginger briefly. **4** Add CHILI JAM, sausage slices, bean sprouts, and scallions and toss over heat. Add duck pieces and cook until heated through, about 90 seconds. Tip into a bowl. **5** Return wok to heat and toss rice noodles with sweet soy and fish sauces over high heat for 2 minutes. **6** Put noodles into the bowl with cooked ingredients and add beaten egg to the wok. As it starts to set, throw the noodles and duck mixture back into the wok and toss so that noodles are coated with egg. **7** Pile noodles onto plates, sprinkle with chives and fried garlic slices, and serve.

*Serves 4*

one 2 lb. (1 kg) piece of pork belly, with skin
4 tsp. sea salt
4 tsp. Chinese Five-spice Powder (page 200)
1 tsp. Sichuan peppercorns, roasted and ground
1 tsp. sesame oil
1 bunch Chinese broccoli (gai lan), washed
3 tbsp. (40 ml) Chinese oyster sauce
4 tsp. CHILI JAM (page 6)

## Five-spice roasted pork belly

**1** Bring a large pot of water to boiling point. Add pork belly and blanch for 3 minutes. Remove from pot and set aside to cool for 10 minutes. **2** Mix salt with five-spice powder and ground pepper. Rub pork with sesame oil, then rub spiced salt liberally into pork, covering all surfaces. Leave at room temperature for 2 hours. **3** Preheat oven to hot at 450°F (220°C). Lay pork belly on a wire rack over a roasting pan that is one-third full of hot water. Place in center of oven and roast for 40 minutes. Reduce heat slightly to 400°F (200°C), toss out water from roasting pan, and continue to dry-roast pork for another 20 minutes, or until it is tender and the skin is crisp. Test with a skewer and, if juices run clear, meat is cooked. Remove pork from the oven and let rest in a warm place for 15 minutes before slicing. **4** Cut broccoli into 2 in. (5 cm) lengths, including stems and leaves, peeling any thick stems if necessary. Cook in boiling water for a few minutes until softened. Remove from water and toss with oyster sauce in a pan over high heat until evenly coated. **5** Lay cooked broccoli on serving plates. Cut pork into thick slices, arrange over broccoli, and serve with CHILI JAM. Sichuan Spice Salt (page 200) and lemon wedges could be served as additional condiments.

*Serves 4*

8 dried Chinese black mushrooms
One 2 lb. (1 kg) piece of pork belly, with skin
2 qt. (2 l) Red Braising Stock (page 203)
vegetable oil, for deep-frying
steamed rice, to serve
4 tsp. CHILI JAM (page 6)
1 bunch Chinese chives, cut into ½ in. (1 cm) lengths

## Red-cooked pork with chili jam

**1** Soak dried mushrooms in boiling water to cover for 30 minutes. Remove from water and cut off stems. Discard water. **2** Meanwhile, cut pork belly into 4 even pieces. Put in a large pot, cover with cold water, and bring to the boil. Simmer for 5 minutes, remove from heat, and drain meat in colander. Rinse thoroughly under cold water. **3** Bring stock to boiling point in a large pot. Add pork, reduce heat, and simmer very gently, stirring occasionally, for 30 minutes. **4** Turn off heat, add softened mushrooms, and leave with pork in stock for a further 20 minutes, or until meat is tender and glossy in appearance. Remove pork and mushrooms from pot with a slotted spoon. Drain on paper towels. **5** Heat oil in a deep-fryer or large pot to 350°F (180°C) and fry pork for 5 minutes, or until outer surfaces are crisp and caramelized in appearance. **6** Slice each piece of pork in half and serve with steamed rice, CHILI JAM, and a sprinkling of chives. Add a spoonful of the pot juices and some steamed green vegetables, if desired.

*Serves 4*

10 shallots, chopped
10 cloves garlic, chopped
2 stalks lemongrass, chopped
4 slices fresh galangal (or ginger), chopped
3 tbsp. (40 ml) vegetable oil
2 tsp. ground turmeric
8 tsp. CHILI JAM (page 6)
4½ lb. (2 kg) oxtail, cut into 1¾ in. (4 cm) pieces
6 ripe tomatoes, quartered
1⅔ cups (400 ml) tomato purée
2 qt. (2 l) White Chicken Stock (page 202) *or* water
2 cups (500 ml) Tamarind Liquid (page 200)
2 oz. (60 g) brown sugar (*or* palm sugar, shaved)
4 large red Anaheim *or* Dutch chilies, split lengthwise
3 kaffir lime leaves
fish sauce
freshly ground black pepper
4 tbsp. Fried Shallot Slices (page 201)
steamed white rice *or* fresh rice noodles, to serve

## Hot-and-sour braised oxtail

**1** Using a food processor or mortar and pestle, blend shallots, garlic, lemongrass, and galangal to a paste with oil, turmeric, and CHILI JAM. Put into a large dish with oxtail pieces, tomato, and tomato purée and marinate for 2 hours or overnight. **2** In a large pot, bring stock to simmering point with tamarind liquid and brown sugar. Add oxtail and its marinade, chilies, and lime leaves. Simmer over low heat, uncovered, for at least 2½ hours or until oxtail is tender and liquid has reduced by about half. The slower the cooking, the better the result. **3** Season to taste with fish sauce and pepper, adding enough of each to balance the flavors. Sprinkle with fried shallot slices and serve with rice or noodles.

*Serves 4*

Note: This dish will develop even more flavor if prepared a day in advance to the point of adding the fish sauce and pepper. Add seasonings and gently reheat over low heat the next day.

# Harissa

Harissa is a staple in the North African, and more specifically the Tunisian, diet. It is used to add both flavor and color to many preparations. Harissa is a counterpart to an Asian sambal, although very much hotter on the palate as it has not been mellowed by cooking or had the addition of sugar. It has a fiery taste and is traditionally served as a condiment, like a relish. It is great with oil and a little lemon juice for dipping bread, for mixing with olives, to enhance salads or soups and cooked fish and meats, as well as being an automatic addition to any couscous preparation. As with all chili preparations, test the water first – taste – and then use harissa accordingly. The heat of the relish can be varied according to the type of dried chilies used in the preparation. I use the larger dried Chinese or New Mexican chilies, but if you want to give it an extra kick, add a few dried Thai or other small Asian chilies, or the fiery habaneros.

2½ oz. (75 g) large dried Anaheim *or* Dutch chilies,
   chopped
2 tsp. cumin seeds
¼ tsp. caraway seeds
2 large cloves garlic, chopped
1 tsp. sea salt
3½ tbsp. (50 ml) tomato purée
¼ cup (60 ml) olive oil

## Harissa

**1** Soak chili in a little water for 2 hours. Drain, reserving soaking water. **2** Dry-roast cumin seeds over gentle heat until fragrant. Cool, then grind to a fine powder with caraway seeds. **3** Blend chili, garlic, and ⅓ cup (100 ml) reserved soaking water in a food processor, then add spices, salt, and tomato purée. With motor running, slowly pour in oil and blend until paste is smooth. **4** Spoon into a sterilized jar, cover with a film of oil, and seal. Keeps, refrigerated, for up to 1 month.

*Makes about 1 cup (250 ml)*

1 bulb garlic

extra-virgin olive oil

4 tomatoes

sea salt

freshly ground black pepper

4¾ cups (1.2 l) White Chicken Stock (page 202)

1¾ cups (400 g) cooked chickpeas

1 tsp. cumin seeds, roasted and ground

4 tsp. HARISSA (page 26)

2 tbsp. finely chopped flat-leaf parsley

1 tbsp. shredded mint leaves

1 tbsp. diced red onion

## Chickpea and harissa soup

**1** Preheat oven to moderate at 350°F (180°C). Cut top off garlic bulb, drizzle with a little olive oil, and wrap in foil. Cut tomatoes in half lengthwise, drizzle with a little olive oil, and season with salt and pepper. **2** Roast garlic and tomatoes for 30 minutes, or until garlic is soft and tomato is soft and colored. Unwrap and squeeze roasted garlic cloves from their skins. Discard skins. **3** In a large pot, bring stock, chickpeas, garlic, and tomato to boiling point. Stir in cumin, 1 tsp. salt, ½ tsp. pepper, and HARISSA and simmer for 10 minutes. Taste and, if necessary, adjust seasoning. **4** Swirl in herbs, diced onion, and 4 tsp. (20 ml) olive oil, and serve soup with crusty bread. Additions can include a poached egg, shredded chicken, or crispy bacon or pancetta strips, depending on your preference.

*Serves 4*

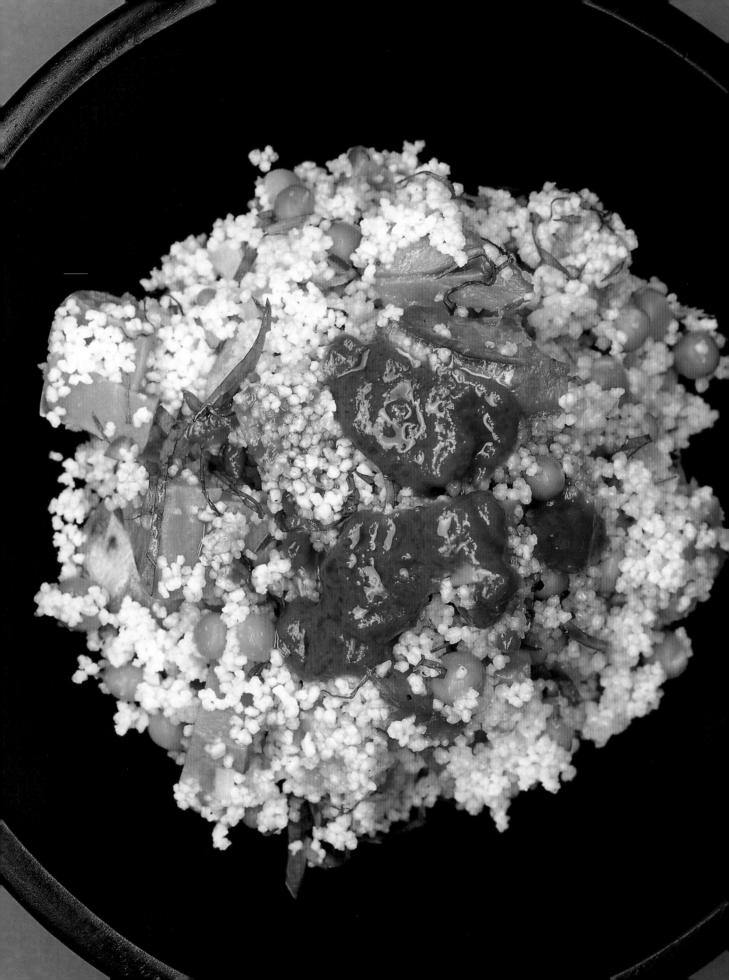

7 oz. (200 g) sweet potato, cut into 1 in. (2.5 cm) dice

7 oz. (200 g) pumpkin, cut into 1 in. (2.5 cm) dice

3 tbsp. (40 ml) olive oil

1 tsp. sea salt

1 tsp. freshly ground black pepper

1¼ cups (300 ml) Spiced Vegetable Stock (page 204)
   *or* water

1 cup (200 g) couscous

4 tbsp. (60 g) unsalted butter

4 oz. (100 g) fresh peas, blanched

1 red onion, finely diced

4 tsp. diced PRESERVED LEMON (page 124)

2 tbsp. shredded mint leaves

4 tsp. HARISSA (page 26)

**Salad dressing**

½ cup (125 ml) extra-virgin olive oil

1 tbsp. (15 ml) red wine vinegar

1 tbsp. (20 ml) lemon juice, strained

sea salt

freshly ground black pepper

## Roasted vegetable and couscous salad

**1** Preheat oven to moderately hot at 400°F (200°C). **2** To make salad dressing, whisk olive oil, vinegar, and lemon juice and season to taste with salt and pepper. **3** Put sweet potato and pumpkin into a roasting tray and add olive oil, salt, and pepper. Bake for 25 minutes, or until golden and soft. Remove from oven and set aside. **4** Bring stock to boiling point in a saucepan and pour in couscous, stirring continuously. Remove from heat, stir in butter, cover pan, and allow to sit for about 15 minutes, or until couscous has absorbed all the liquid. Fluff with a fork. **5** Put couscous into a large bowl and stir through baked vegetables, peas, onion, PRESERVED LEMON, and mint. **6** Spoon salad onto plates, drizzle with dressing, and add a teaspoon of HARISSA to each serving.

*Serves 4*

## Vegetable hotpot

4 tsp. (20 ml) olive oil

1 medium onion, quartered

2 tbsp. diced red bell pepper

2 cloves garlic, finely chopped

2 tsp. ras el hanout spice mix

2 tsp. HARISSA (page 26)

6 cups (1.5 l) Spiced Vegetable Stock (page 204)

2 potatoes, peeled and cut into eighths

1 turnip, peeled and cut into eighths

1 parsnip, peeled and cut into thick rounds

2 zucchini, cut into 2 in. (5 cm) lengths

4 broccoli florets

4 tomatoes, quartered

4 tsp. (20 ml) lemon juice

2 tsp. sea salt

1 tsp. freshly ground black pepper

3 tbsp. cilantro leaves

2 tbsp. shredded mint leaves

couscous *or* steamed rice, to serve

**1** Heat oil in a large frying pan and fry onion, bell pepper, and garlic until softened. Add ras el hanout and HARISSA and fry for another 3 minutes, or until fragrant. **2** Add stock and bring to simmering point. Add potato and turnip and simmer for 15 minutes. Add remaining vegetables and simmer for another 25 minutes, or until vegetables are soft and cooked. **3** Add lemon juice and season with salt and pepper. Remove from heat and stir in herbs. **4** Serve with couscous or rice. Extra HARISSA can be served as a condiment, if desired.

*Serves 4*

2 cooked chicken breasts

10 oz. (300 g) short pasta (penne, rigatoni *or* spirals)

sea salt

⅓ cup (80 ml) extra-virgin olive oil

1 medium onion, finely sliced

4 cloves garlic, finely chopped

2 small Thai *or* serrano chilies, seeded and
    finely chopped

2 teaspoons HARISSA (page 26)

¾ cup roasted-tomato pasta sauce (any commercially
    available brand)

½ tsp. freshly ground black pepper

½ cup finely chopped flat-leaf parsley

¼ lb. (100 g) feta cheese, diced (see Note)

Pasta with chicken, feta, and harissa

**1** Julienne the chicken and set aside. **2** Bring a pot of water to the boil, add pasta and 1 tsp. sea salt, and cook until pasta is al dente. Strain. **3** While pasta is cooking, heat olive oil in a frying pan and fry onion until it starts to color. Add garlic and chilies and cook for 1 minute, or until fragrant. **4** Add HARISSA and tomato pasta sauce and cook for 5 minutes on moderate heat. Season with salt and pepper. Stir in chicken and simmer for about 2 minutes, or until meat has heated through. Remove from heat. **5** Toss chicken mixture, parsley, and feta through pasta and serve immediately.

*Serves 4*

Note: Ricotta can be substituted for feta.

## Spiced ratatouille

one 10 oz. (300 g) eggplant, cut into
   ¾ in. (2 cm) cubes
sea salt
⅓ cup (100 ml) olive oil
1 medium onion, diced
3 cloves garlic, finely chopped
½ tsp. ground coriander
½ tsp. ground cumin
2 red bell peppers, seeded and cut into
   ¾ in. (2 cm) pieces
4 small zucchini, diced
4 tomatoes, peeled and diced
2 tsp. HARISSA (page 26)
¼ cup finely chopped flat-leaf parsley
freshly ground black pepper

**1** Lay eggplant on a tray in a single layer and salt lightly. Leave for 30 minutes, then rub off salt and excess liquid with a paper towel. **2** Heat oil in a large lidded frying pan and gently fry onion, garlic, and spices until fragrant. **3** Add eggplant and bell pepper, cover with lid and cook over low heat for 25 minutes, or until very soft. **4** Add zucchini and tomato and cook, covered, for a further 15 minutes. **5** Stir in HARISSA and parsley and season to taste with salt and pepper. Serve hot, warm, or at room temperature with grilled meats or fish, or as a starter with crusty bread.

*Serves 4*

Duck and lemon risotto with harissa

one 5 lb. (2.3 kg) duck, roasted *or* braised
4¾ cups (1.2 l) White Chicken Stock (page 202)
1 tbsp. unsalted butter
3 tbsp. (40 ml) fruity extra-virgin olive oil
1 large onion, diced
4 cloves garlic, minced
1 fennel bulb, diced
zest of 2 lemons, blanched and minced
2¼ cups (400 g) arborio rice
½ cup (125 ml) white wine
1 tbsp. (20 ml) lemon juice
1 tsp. sea salt
½ tsp. freshly ground black pepper
½ cup lemon basil *or* basil leaves, torn
4 tsp. HARISSA (page 26)

**1** Using your fingers, shred meat from duck and set aside. Discard skin, fat, and bones. **2** Bring stock to boiling point, then reduce heat to a low simmer. **3** Heat butter and oil in a wide-based pan and fry onion, garlic, and fennel until softened and beginning to color. Add lemon zest. Stir in rice and fry gently until it is well coated with the aromatics. Add wine and cook over medium heat until wine has been absorbed. Stirring continuously, gradually add hot stock, a ladleful at a time, adding each new ladleful when the last one has been absorbed. By the last ladleful, the rice should be nearly cooked – this will take about 20 minutes. **4** With the last application of stock, stir through shredded duck meat and lemon juice. Season and cook for 2 to 3 minutes. Remove from heat and stir lemon basil leaves through. Serve immediately with HARISSA as a condiment.

*Serves 4*

4 tsp. (20 ml) olive oil

8 lamb shanks

8 spring onions, white bulbs only, peeled

8 cloves garlic

2 small Thai *or* serrano chilies, sliced

¾ cup (200 ml) red wine

4¾ cups (1.2 l) Beef/Veal Stock (page 203)
   *or* Brown Chicken Stock (page 202)

2 sprigs of rosemary

1 bay leaf

3¼ cups (800 ml) water

1 cup (170 g) polenta

½ stick (50 g) unsalted butter

1 tsp. sea salt

1 tsp. freshly ground black pepper

1 tsp. ground chili *or* paprika

8 tsp. HARISSA (page 26)

# Slow-cooked lamb shanks with polenta and harissa

**1** Preheat oven to moderately low at 325°F (160°C). Heat oil in a large heavy-bottomed roasting pan and fry shanks on all sides for about 10 minutes, or until brown. Remove from pan and set aside. **2** In the same roasting pan, fry spring onion bulbs, garlic, and chilies for a few minutes. Add wine and bring to the boil. Cook for 5 minutes, then add stock, rosemary, and bay leaf. **3** Bring to the boil, reduce heat to a simmer, and return shanks to pan. Cover and cook in oven for 2 hours. **4** While shanks are cooking, prepare polenta. Bring water to the boil in a large saucepan and pour in polenta. Reduce heat to low and whisk to combine. Cook polenta over heat, stirring, for 25 to 30 minutes, or until done. (It is cooked when it comes away cleanly from sides of pan and appears homogenous.) If it gets too dry and stiff during cooking, add a little more water. Stir in butter and season with salt, pepper, and ground chili. Remove from heat. **5** Remove shanks, onions, and garlic from tray with a slotted spoon and keep warm. **6** Pour stock into a saucepan and boil over high heat until reduced by half. Strain through a fine mesh sieve. Stir half the HARISSA into the smooth sauce. **7** Spoon soft polenta onto plates and sit lamb shanks, onions, and garlic on top. Ladle some sauce over and add a teaspoon of the remaining HARISSA to each serving.

*Serves 4*

8 lemon slices

4 sprigs of dill

4 whole, plate-size fish (red snapper, rouget, catfish,
    cod, etc.), cleaned, scaled, and rinsed

1 tsp. sea salt

1 tsp. freshly ground black pepper

3 tbsp. (40 ml) extra-virgin olive oil

2 tsp. HARISSA (page 26)

2 tsp. lemon juice

vegetable oil, for deep-frying basil leaves

½ cup basil leaves

# Grilled fish with harissa dressing

**1** Put 2 lemon slices and 1 sprig of dill in cavity of each fish. Season fish liberally with salt and pepper. Drizzle 2 tbsp. olive oil over fish to prevent sticking during cooking and place fish on a sheet pan. **2** Mix HARISSA with the remaining olive oil and the lemon juice. **3** Heat some vegetable oil in a deep-fryer or saucepan to 350°F (180°C) and deep-fry basil leaves for about 20 seconds, or until crisp. Drain on paper towels. **4** Cook fish under a griller for 6 minutes, then flip over and cook for another 3 to 5 minutes, depending on thickness. Flesh should be white and firm without being dry or breaking open. **5** Remove lemon and dill from cavity and spoon HARISSA dressing over fish. Sprinkle with deep-fried basil leaves to serve.

*Serves 4*

olive oil

4 medium onions, sliced

6 cloves garlic, finely sliced

1 tsp. cumin seeds, roasted and ground

6 ripe tomatoes, peeled and quartered *or*
  one 12 oz. (400 g) can tomatoes, drained

2 tbsp. chopped oregano

1 tsp. sea salt

1 tsp. freshly ground black pepper

8 spicy lamb Merguez *or* other sausages

4 tsp. HARISSA (page 26)

## Spicy sausages with onion, tomato, and harissa

**1** Preheat oven to 450°F (220°C). **2** Heat oil in a frying pan and fry onion, garlic, and cumin over moderate heat for 10 minutes, or until starting to color. Stir in tomatoes and cook, covered, for another 15 minutes, or until tomatoes start to lose their form. Stir in oregano and season with salt and pepper. **3** Grill sausages for about 10 minutes, or until brown on all sides. Transfer to oven to cook for a further 5 to 6 minutes. **4** Serve sausages with tomato mixture, HARISSA, and crusty bread.

*Serves 4*

3 tbsp. (40 ml) olive oil

8 tsp. HARISSA (page 26)

one 1¼ lb. (600 g) beef tenderloin

extra HARISSA, to serve

**Bean salad**

½ cup (125 ml) extra-virgin olive oil

1 small onion, diced

2 cloves garlic, finely chopped

1 small Thai *or* serrano chili, seeded and

   finely chopped

2 tsp. ground cumin

½ cup (100 g) green Puy lentils, washed

¾ cup (200 ml) White Chicken Stock (page 202)

   *or* water

½ cup (100 g) green beans, sliced

½ cup (100 g) butter beans, sliced

½ cup (100 g) fava beans (broad beans), peeled

2 tbsp. (30 ml) red wine vinegar

1 tsp. sea salt

1 tsp. freshly ground black pepper

½ cup chopped chervil *or* flat-leaf parsley

# Grilled beef with bean salad and harissa

**1** Preheat oven to 450°F (220°C). **2** To make bean salad, heat 4 tsp. of the oil and fry onion, garlic, and chili until beginning to color. Add cumin and lentils and fry for another minute or two. Add stock and cook over low heat for about 20 minutes, or until lentils are soft and liquid has been absorbed. Remove from heat. **3** Cook green beans, butter beans, and fava beans in boiling salted water for 2 minutes, or until al dente. Strain and rinse under cold water to refresh and maintain color. Add cooked beans to lentils. **4** Whisk vinegar and remaining olive oil in a bowl and season with salt and pepper. Dress beans with vinaigrette and add chervil. **5** To cook beef, rub olive oil and HARISSA over meat to coat thoroughly. Heat a grill pan and sear meat on all sides for about 10 minutes, or until browned. Transfer to a sheet pan and cook in oven for 8 minutes. At this stage, the meat should be medium-rare, quite pink in the center and maintaining maximum moisture. Remove from oven and rest for 10 minutes before slicing. **6** Spoon bean salad onto a large plate. Slice beef and arrange on top of salad. Serve with extra HARISSA and crusty bread.

*Serves 4*

Note: Instead of pan grilling, the meat can be barbecued over hot coals for 10 to 15 minutes and then rested in a warm place for 15 minutes.

## Sambal Bajak

By their very nature, all sambals should be slightly fiery on the palate. Because it is a cooked preparation, this sambal is more gentle, relatively speaking, than the raw varieties (sambal olek) that are commercially available. Sambal bajak includes onions for sweetness and shrimp paste and tamarind for sourness and depth of flavor. Used mainly in Indonesian cooking and popular with rice dishes such as Nasi Goreng, it is made with the milder, large Lombok or Chinese chilies. Any sambal preparation can be served as a condiment or an accompaniment to a main dish, where its piquancy lifts the flavor of the food. Having a range of sambals at hand means that you can transform ordinary food in a flash. Like CHILI JAM, this sambal is partnered by and compatible with other pastes throughout this book.

## Sambal bajak

2 tbsp. (30 g) Malaysian shrimp paste (belacan)
20 large red Anaheim *or* Dutch chilies, chopped
6 macadamia nuts
4 tsp. finely chopped ginger
4 tsp. finely chopped garlic
10 shallots, sliced
6 kaffir lime leaves, slivered
4 tbsp. (50 ml) vegetable oil
2 tbsp. (30 ml) Tamarind Liquid (page 200)
1 cup (250 ml) coconut milk
1 tbsp. (30 g) brown sugar (*or* palm sugar, shaved)
3 tbsp. (40 ml) fish sauce

**1** Dry-roast shrimp paste over gentle heat until fragrant. Blend shrimp paste, chilies, macadamia nuts, ginger, garlic, shallots, lime leaves, and oil to a smooth paste in a food processor. **2** Cook paste over gentle heat for 10 to 15 minutes, or until softened. Add remaining ingredients and bring to the boil. Simmer for 30 minutes until a thick paste has formed and a layer of oil is evident. **3** Stir oil back into sambal and remove from heat. Spoon into a sterilized jar and seal when cool. Keeps, refrigerated, for up to 2 months.

*Makes about 1¼ cups (300 ml)*

½ tbsp. raw peanuts

1 tsp. chili oil

½ clove garlic, sliced

½ tsp. finely chopped ginger

¼ large red Anaheim *or* Dutch chili, cut into julienne

¼ red bell pepper, cut into julienne

½ scallion, cut into 1 in. (2.5 cm) lengths

¼ small carrot, cut into julienne

¼ zucchini, cut into julienne

2 snow peas, cut into julienne

½ Chinese long bean, cut into 2 in. (5 cm) lengths
  and blanched

2 oyster mushrooms, halved

½ bok choy leaf, coarsely shredded

⅛ cup (30 g) bean sprouts

4 tsp. (20 ml) Tamarind Liquid (page 200)

½ tsp. sugar

½ tsp. fish sauce

1 tsp. sweet soy sauce (kecap manis)

1 tsp. SAMBAL BAJAK (page 42)

½ cup small tatsoi leaves *or* watercress sprigs

½ large hard-boiled egg

## Stir-fried chili vegetables with roasted peanuts

**1** Dry-roast peanuts over low heat until colored and fragrant. Cool and chop roughly. Set aside. **2** Heat a wok, add chili oil, and fry garlic, ginger, and chili for 1 minute, or until fragrant. Add bell pepper, scallion, carrot, zucchini, snow peas, Chinese long bean, and mushrooms and toss over heat for 1 to 2 minutes, or until vegetables start to wilt. Add bok choy and bean sprouts with tamarind liquid, sugar, fish sauce, soy sauce, and SAMBAL BAJAK. Toss to combine. Stir tatsoi through hot vegetables and remove wok from heat. **3** Pile stir-fried vegetables on a plate, top with egg, and sprinkle with roasted peanuts. Serve immediately.
*Serves 1*

Note: If making this dish for more than 1 person, cook each serving separately for best results. If Chinese long beans are unavailable, regular green beans can be substituted.

4 tsp. (20 ml) vegetable oil
2 cloves garlic, finely chopped
1 small Thai *or* serrano chili, finely chopped
2 tsp. fish sauce
4 tsp. Chinese oyster sauce
2 tsp. Chinese black vinegar
1 tsp. sweet soy sauce (kecap manis)
7 oz. (200 g) green beans, trimmed
4 tsp. SAMBAL BAJAK (page 42)
4 scallions, finely sliced

## Green bean sambal

**1** Heat oil in a wok, add garlic, chili, fish sauce, oyster sauce, vinegar, sweet soy sauce, and green beans. Toss over heat and cook for 2 minutes, or until beans begin to soften. **2** Stir in SAMBAL BAJAK and cook for another minute to coat beans with paste. Add a little water to prevent burning. **3** Remove from heat, add sliced scallion, and serve.

*Serves 4*

Note: Thin asparagus can be substituted for beans.

## Spiced coconut fish soup

4 tsp. (20 ml) vegetable oil

2 stalks lemongrass, chopped

4 kaffir lime leaves, chopped

zest of 2 limes

2 small Thai *or* serrano chillies, sliced

3 tsp. finely chopped ginger

2 cilantro roots, finely chopped

4 scallions, sliced

4 tsp. SAMBAL BAJAK (page 42)

1⅔ cups (400 ml) Fish Stock (page 201)

3⅓ cups (800 ml) coconut milk

2 tsp. strained lime juice

4 tsp. (20 ml) fish sauce

7 oz. (200 g) fish fillets, cut into chunks

¼ cup fresh cilantro leaves

¼ cup shredded mint leaves

**1** Heat oil in a pot and fry lemongrass, lime leaves, half the lime zest, chilies, ginger, cilantro root, and scallions for about 4 minutes, or until softened. Add SAMBAL BAJAK and fry for another minute. Add stock and coconut milk and bring to the boil. Reduce heat and simmer for 20 minutes. **2** Strain soup through a fine mesh sieve, discarding solids. Return soup to pot and flavor with lime juice and fish sauce. **3** Poach fish chunks in soup over gentle heat for 3 minutes. Ladle fish and soup into bowls and add remaining lime rind, cilantro leaves, and mint leaves.

*Serves 4*

Note: For variety, use Shrimp Stock (page 202) in place of Fish Stock and add shellfish to the broth as well as some fish.

3 tbsp. all-purpose flour

½ tsp. sea salt

½ tsp. freshly ground black pepper

½ tsp. ground chili *or* paprika

1⅓ lb. (600 g) fresh whitebait, washed and
  dried on paper towels

vegetable oil, for deep-frying

8 tsp. SAMBAL BAJAK (page 42)

4 lemon wedges

## Fried whitebait with chili

**1** Season flour with salt, pepper, and chili. Coat whitebait with seasoned flour. **2** Heat oil to 350°F (180°C) in deep-fryer or large pot. Cook whitebait in small batches for 1 minute, or until crisp. Drain on paper towels. **3** Serve with SAMBAL BAJAK and lemon wedges.

*Serves 4*

3 tbsp. (40 ml) vegetable oil
2 cloves garlic, finely chopped
8 tsp. SAMBAL BAJAK (page 42)
2 lb. (1 kg) small green tiger or white shrimp,
washed (see Note)

## Chili shrimp

**1** Heat oil in a wok and fry garlic and SAMBAL BAJAK for a minute. **2** Add shrimp and toss over high heat to coat them with chili. Cook until shrimp are crisp and have changed to a bright pink color. Serve immediately. These shrimps are meant to be devoured in their entirety, heads and all. Have an ample supply of napkins on hand.

*Serves 4*

Note: Larger shrimp can be used in this recipe, but discard the heads before cooking and remove the tough shells before eating.

4 tsp. (20 ml) strained lime juice

½ tsp. freshly ground white pepper

4 tsp. SAMBAL BAJAK (page 42)

16 green tiger *or* white shrimp, shelled
and deveined

2 tsp. vegetable oil

½ cup (125 ml) canned coconut cream

2 tsp. fish sauce

1 tbsp. finely shredded mint leaves

2 tsp. Fried Shallot Slices (page 201)

## Shrimp sambal

**1** Combine lime juice, pepper, and SAMBAL BAJAK in a bowl. Add shrimp and coat thoroughly with paste. **2** Heat oil in a wok or heavy-based pan and fry shrimp over moderately high heat for 2 minutes to seal in juices. **3** Add coconut cream and fish sauce and stir to combine. Cook for 2 minutes only. **4** Remove from heat, garnish with shredded mint and fried shallot slices, and serve with salad or rice.

*Serves 4*

¾ lb. (400 g) cleaned squid bodies (see Note)
4 tsp. SAMBAL BAJAK (page 42)
2 tsp. strained lime juice
2 tsp. fish sauce
4 tsp. (20 ml) vegetable oil
⅓ cup (80 ml) Sweet Chili Sauce (page 200)
1 small cucumber, finely sliced
⅔ cup (150 g) bean sprouts
2 scallions, finely sliced
¼ cup shredded mint leaves
¼ cup cilantro leaves
1 large red Anaheim *or* Dutch Chili, finely sliced

# Chili squid salad

**1** Cut squid bodies in half lengthwise and carefully score inner flesh diagonally. Combine squid, SAMBAL BAJAK, lime juice, and fish sauce in a bowl. **2** Heat oil in a wok or pan and fry squid over high heat for 2 minutes, or until just cooked. It will curl as it cooks because of the scoring, which also helps to keep it tender. **3** Remove from heat, toss with sweet chili sauce and remaining salad ingredients, and serve.

*Serves 4*

Note: Cuttlefish or small octopus can just as easily be used in this preparation.

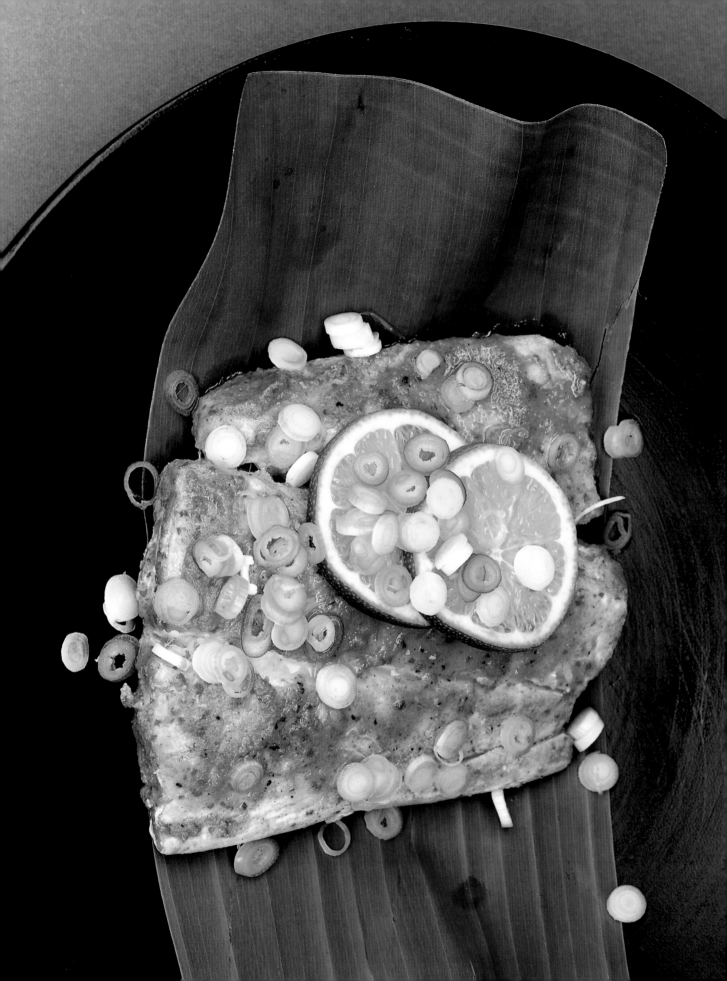

4 tbsp. SAMBAL BAJAK (page 42)

4 fresh banana leaves, cut into large squares (see Note)

four 5 oz. (150 g) white fish fillets (snapper, barramundi,
    grouper, sea bass, halibut, mackerel, etc.)

½ tsp. sea salt

½ tsp. freshly ground black pepper

3 tbsp. (40 ml) strained lime juice

scallions, finely sliced

slices of lime

steamed rice, to serve

## Chili fish baked in banana leaf

1 Spoon 2 tsp. SAMBAL BAJAK onto each banana leaf. Lay each fish fillet on a banana leaf and season with salt, pepper, and lime juice. Spoon remaining SAMBAL BAJAK over fish and fold banana leaf over to cover the fish and make a package. Secure with skewers or toothpicks. 2 Cook fish parcels over a charcoal grill or in a moderate oven at 350°F (180°C) for 5 to 6 minutes each side (10 to 12 minutes total, or longer if necessary, depending on the thickness and density of the fish). 3 Remove fish parcels from heat, unwrap, and discard banana leaves. Scatter scallions over the fish and add a slice or two of lime, if desired. Serve with steamed rice.

*Serves 4*

Note: Banana leaves can be purchased frozen if fresh leaves are unavailable.

## Chili soy chicken with sesame noodles

2 tsp. white sesame seeds

vegetable oil

8 cloves garlic

3 qt. (3 l) Red Braising Stock (page 203)

4 chicken thighs, cut in half at the joint

1 tsp. Sichuan Spice Salt (page 200)

4 Japanese eggplants

8 oz. (250 g) somen noodles

¼ cup shredded spearmint leaves

2 tbsp. torn basil leaves

2 scallions, finely sliced

2 cups watercress sprigs

**Sesame soy dressing**

3 tbsp. (40 ml) soy sauce

2 tsp. sesame oil

4 tsp. SAMBAL BAJAK (page 42)

3 tbsp. (40 ml) lemon juice, strained

3½ tbsp. (50 ml) Chinese rice vinegar

¼ cup (60 ml) mirin

¼ cup (60 ml) Sugar Syrup (page 201) *or*
  2 tbsp. sugar

4 cloves garlic, finely chopped

**1** Dry-roast sesame seeds in a frying pan over gentle heat until just colored. Cool and set aside. **2** Heat oil and shallow-fry garlic cloves until golden and softened. Drain on paper towel. **3** To make dressing, combine all ingredients. Set aside. **4** Bring stock to the boil in a stockpot. Put chicken pieces into stock, turn off heat, and let chicken cook gently in hot stock for 30 minutes. Check that meat is cooked by testing each piece with a metal skewer – if juices run pale pink, chicken is ready. Leave a little longer if juices are too pink. **5** Remove cooked chicken from stock and cut meat into strips or shred with fingers, discarding bones. Sprinkle with Sichuan spice salt. **6** Quarter eggplants lengthwise, score flesh, and brush with oil. Grill until softened and golden brown. **7** Cook noodles in boiling water for 2 minutes, or until soft. Drain and refresh under cold running water. Put noodles into a bowl with half the dressing. **8** In another bowl, mix garlic with herbs, scallions, and watercress. Add chicken and spoon in enough dressing to coat leaves and meat lightly. **9** Pile noodles on plates and sit 2 grilled eggplant halves on each serving. Arrange chicken and salad on top of eggplant and drizzle with a little extra dressing. Sprinkle with sesame seeds and serve immediately.

*Serves 4*

vegetable oil, for deep-frying

2 lb. (1 kg) pork spareribs, trimmed and cut into
single ribs, on the bone

1 qt. (1 l) White Chicken Stock (page 202)

4 cloves garlic, finely chopped

4 slices ginger

4 scallions, chopped

8 tsp. SAMBAL BAJAK (page 42)

4 tsp. (20 ml) Chinese yellow bean sauce

4 tsp. (20 ml) light soy sauce

2 tsp. sweet soy sauce (kecap manis)

1 tbsp. brown sugar (*or* palm sugar, shaved)

3 tbsp. (40 ml) Chinese Shaoxing rice wine

2 tsp. fish sauce

steamed Chinese broccoli (gai lan), to serve

# Chili pork spareribs

1 Heat oil to 350°F (180°C) in a deep-fryer or large pot and deep-fry spareribs, a few at a time, for 5 minutes until brown. Drain on paper towels. 2 Heat stock with remaining ingredients, except Chinese broccoli, to boiling point in a large saucepan. Reduce heat to a simmer, add spareribs, and simmer over low heat for 1 hour. 3 Preheat oven to 400°F (200°C). Remove ribs from stock and lay on a wire rack placed over a roasting pan. Bake for 10 minutes, or until crisp. Serve with Chinese broccoli and extra SAMBAL BAJAK as a condiment.

*Serves 4*

1½ oz. (50 g) dried rice vermicelli (beehoon)

24 cooked yabby tails, peeled (see Note)

twelve 6 in. (16 cm) square rice paper sheets

1 cup bean sprouts, blanched

½ cup snow pea sprouts

2 tbsp. finely grated carrot

2 tbsp. shredded cucumber

2 tbsp. Vietnamese mint (laksa) leaves

2 tbsp. cilantro leaves

4 tsp. SAMBAL BAJAK (page 42)

**Sweet chili and peanut dipping sauce**

½ cup (125 ml) lime juice

¼ cup (60 ml) fish sauce

3 tbsp. (40 ml) rice vinegar *or* coconut vinegar

3 tbsp. sugar

2 cloves garlic, minced

2 Thai chilies, minced

1 tbsp. crushed roasted peanuts

# Rice paper rolls with shellfish and chili

**1** To make the dipping sauce, combine all ingredients except peanuts. Taste and adjust seasoning if necessary. Set aside. **2** Soak vermicelli in warm water for 30 minutes, then cook in boiling water for 2 minutes, or until soft. Drain and refresh with cold water. Drain again and set aside. Cut yabby tails in half lengthwise and devein. **3** Set out all ingredients on work surface, with a large bowl of hot water alongside. Lay a clean, folded tea towel next to the bowl. **4** Working with 1 sheet of rice paper at a time, soften each sheet in hot water for 30 seconds. Lift from water and place on folded cloth. Lay a few vermicelli noodles on rice paper, about a third up from base and spreading them two-thirds of the way across the sheet. **5** On top of noodles, place bean sprouts, snow pea sprouts, carrot, and cucumber, then Vietnamese mint and cilantro leaves. Lay 4 yabby tail halves along the top and spread with a little SAMBAL BAJAK. **6** Roll sheet over filling, carefully tucking in the ends to secure. Roll over firmly to make neat, uniform rolls. As you complete each roll, set it on a plate, seam-side down. Continue until all ingredients have been used. **7** Add crushed peanuts to dipping sauce and serve rolls immediately with sauce.

*Makes 12*

Note: If yabby tails are not available, use shrimp, crayfish, lobster tails, or even freshly picked crabmeat.

# Spiced Eggplant Pickle

I have read somewhere that the people of India refer to their pickles and chutneys as "tongue touchers," which I think is a most apt description, evocative of their nature and necessity for inclusion in the ritual of everyday eating. Pickles – cooked preparations where vegetables or fruit are sharpened with vinegar and made fiery with assorted spices – give unparalleled diversity and sensuality to food. For those who appreciate the taste of preserves, this rich, vibrant and spicy pickle is an absolute essential in the larder. It can be served with curries, dosas (rice pancakes) or parathas (flaky Indian bread), or as an accompaniment to cold meats, grilled fish or seafood. It can also be used as a base for other preparations. A small quantity can go a long way.

6 large dried Anaheim *or* Dutch chilies

4 tsp. finely chopped garlic

2 tsp. finely chopped ginger

1 tsp. ground turmeric

4 tsp. brown *or* Chinese mustard seeds

1 lb. (500 g) small eggplants, washed

¾ cup (200 ml) vegetable oil

¼ cup (60 g) brown sugar (*or* palm sugar, shaved)

2 tsp. sea salt

⅓ cup (100 ml) malt vinegar

1 tsp. Garam Masala (page 200)

## Spiced eggplant pickle

**1** Soak chilies in hot water for about 30 minutes, or until soft. Drain, reserving water. In a food processor, blend chilies, garlic, ginger, turmeric, and mustard seeds to a paste with a little reserved soaking water. **2** Slice eggplants into rounds ½ in. (1 cm) thick. **3** Heat oil in a frying pan, then add spice paste and stir for a few minutes to release flavors. Add eggplant and cook, stirring occasionally, until soft. Add brown sugar, salt, and vinegar and simmer over low heat until thick. Remove from heat and stir in garam masala. Cool. **4** Spoon into sterilized jars, cover with a film of oil, and seal. Keeps, refrigerated, for 2 months.

*Makes about 2 cups (500 ml)*

ghee

½ tsp. brown *or* Chinese mustard seeds

20 fresh curry leaves

2 large dried Anaheim *or* New Mexican red chilies

2 small onions, finely sliced

1 tsp. finely chopped ginger

2 small Thai *or* serrano chilies, split lengthwise

4 tsp. mild curry powder

1 tsp. ground turmeric

¾ cup (200 ml) coconut milk

¾ cup (200 ml) water

13 oz. (400 g) potatoes, peeled and cut into 1 in. (2.5 cm) dice

3 tomatoes, peeled and quartered

4 tbsp. cooked peas

1 tsp. sea salt

8 tsp. SPICED EGGPLANT PICKLE (page 60)

**Coconut flatbread**

2 cups (300 g) all-purpose flour

2 tbsp. rice flour

1 cup (250 ml) lukewarm water

2 tbsp. dried coconut

1 tsp. finely chopped green jalapeño chili

2 tsp. finely chopped ginger

1 tsp. sea salt

## Potato curry with Indian-style flatbread and spiced eggplant pickle

**1** Heat 1 tbsp. ghee in a pan and cook mustard seeds, curry leaves, and dried chilies for 30 seconds, or until seeds pop. Stir in onion, ginger, and fresh chilies and cook for about 2 minutes, or until softened. Add curry powder and turmeric and stir to coat onion. Pour in coconut milk and water and bring to a simmer. **2** Add potato and tomato and cook over low heat for 20 minutes, or until potato is soft. Add peas and season to taste with salt. Remove from heat and reheat gently when ready to serve. **3** To make flatbread, sift flours into a bowl. Slowly stir in water to make a smooth batter. Mix in coconut, chili, ginger, and salt. **4** Heat a flat griddle or frying pan, add a little ghee, and pour in enough batter to cover base, turning pan to coat base evenly. Cook flatbread over moderate heat for 3 to 4 minutes, then flip over and cook the other side for another 3 minutes, or until golden. Repeat process until all batter is used. **5** Serve hot flatbread and curry with SPICED EGGPLANT PICKLE as a condiment.

*Serves 4*

Note: If you don't have time to make the flatbread, order some naan bread or parathas from your nearest Indian takeout, or serve the curry and pickle with rice and pappadams. This preparation is known as Masala Dosa.

2 cups (500 ml) thick plain yogurt
vegetable oil, for deep-frying
2 eggplants, cut into ½ in. (1 cm) dice
8 tsp. SPICED EGGPLANT PICKLE (page 60)
2 tsp. fish sauce
¼ cup chopped cilantro leaves

## Spiced eggplant pickle and yogurt salad

**1** Spoon yogurt into a strainer lined with cheesecloth and hang overnight to remove excess moisture. **2** To prepare salad, heat oil to 350°F (180°C) in a deep-fryer or large pot and fry eggplant until golden. Drain on paper towels. **3** Mix eggplant in a bowl with remaining ingredients. Cover and refrigerate until ready to use. Serve with prawn or vegetable pakoras or with grilled spicy fish fillets, or wrap in flatbread (mountain bread, soft tortilla, Lebanese, or Turkish bread) with grilled lamb or chicken as a variation to a regular lunch sandwich.

*Serves 4*

## Pumpkin and pickled eggplant samosas

ten 8 in. (20 cm) square spring roll wrappers
1 egg white
vegetable oil, for deep-frying
**Filling**
2 tbsp. ghee
2 cloves garlic, finely chopped
1 tsp. finely chopped ginger
2 small Thai *or* serrano chilies, finely chopped
7 oz. (200 g) pumpkin, cut into ¼ in. (6 mm) dice
7 oz. (200 g) eggplants, cut into ¼ in. (6 mm) dice
2 tsp. sea salt
8 tsp. SPICED EGGPLANT PICKLE (page 60)
2 tbsp. chopped cilantro leaves

**1** To make filling, heat ghee in a frying pan over moderate heat and cook garlic, ginger, and chilies for 1 minute. Add pumpkin and eggplant and cook for another 8 to 10 minutes, or until pumpkin has softened. Season to taste with salt and stir in SPICED EGGPLANT PICKLE. Remove from heat, allow mixture to cool, then add cilantro. **2** To assemble pastries, cut each wrapper into 3 strips lengthwise, giving you 30 rectangular strips. Place 1 large tsp. of filling mixture on bottom left corner of each strip and fold over and over to wrap into a triangular shape. Brush the last ¼ in. (6 mm) of pastry with egg white and seal. Lay prepared pastries on a tray in a single layer until ready to cook. **3** To cook pastries, heat vegetable oil to 350°F (180°C) in a deep-fryer or large pot and fry, a few at a time, for 4 minutes or until crisp and golden. Remove from oil with a slotted spoon and drain on paper towels. Serve hot with a yogurt-based dipping sauce.

*Makes 30*

4 chicken thigh fillets, skin removed
1 tsp. Garam Masala (page 200)
2 cloves garlic, minced
4 tsp. (20 ml) lime juice
1 tsp. sea salt
1 tsp. freshly ground black pepper
3 tbsp. (40 ml) vegetable oil
4 flatbreads (see Note)
4 tsp. SPICED EGGPLANT PICKLE (page 60)
1 small cucumber, seeded and finely diced
1 small red onion, finely diced
¾ cup (200 g) thick plain yogurt
2 tbsp. shredded mint

## Chicken kebab and eggplant pickle wraps

**1** Soak 8 wooden skewers in water for 1 hour (to prevent them burning during cooking). **2** Cut chicken into 1¼ in. (3 cm) cubes. Mix garam masala, garlic, lime juice, salt, and pepper with oil. Marinate chicken in spiced oil for 30 minutes before cooking. **3** Thread chicken cubes onto skewers. Cook for 5 minutes over hot coals on a barbecue or in a hot skillet. Carefully turn skewers over and cook for a further 3 to 4 minutes or until chicken is cooked and tender. Remove from heat. **4** Grill flatbreads for 2 minutes or until warm and softened. Lay on work surface and spread with eggplant pickle. Remove chicken from skewers and arrange down center of bread (2 skewers per flatbread). Add cucumber and onion. Spoon over some yogurt and sprinkle with mint. Wrap breads up and serve immediately.

*Serves 4*

Note: Any flatbread will do for this dish – pita, roti, naan, lavash, enchilada, or tortilla. Use whichever you prefer and have easy access to.

# Laksa Paste

While we may all be familiar with laksa as a soup, we may not be fully aware of the different varieties that are on offer at the source or home of origin. These soups can be based on coconut milk like those from Malacca, or tamarind like those of Penang or Ipoh. The characteristics of a laksa change according to how it is made, the type of noodles used and the ingredients that are added for serving. A flavorful stock is as important as the quality of the laksa paste. From there, you can create culinary nirvana. This delicious, addictive paste is an absolute essential in your pantry. Originating in Malaysia and of Nonya origin, its authentic flavor is second to none. It can also be used as a stir-fry paste, a marinade for grilled foods or a curry paste, or it can be added to pickles or chutneys for greater depth of flavor.

## Laksa paste

1 tsp. (5 g) dried Thai chilies
4 tbsp. (60 g) Malaysian shrimp paste (belacan)
4 tsp. (20 g) dried shrimp
1 tbsp. (15 g) ground turmeric
2 tsp. (10 g) coriander seeds, roasted and ground
4 oz. (125 g) fresh lemongrass stalks, finely sliced
3 oz. (90 g) fresh galangal *or* ginger, chopped
2½ oz. (75 g) fresh turmeric, chopped (see Note)
1½ oz. (50 g) Thai chilies
5 oz. (150 g) shallots, finely sliced
5 oz. (150 g) garlic cloves
3½ oz. (100 g) macadamia nuts
2 cups (500 ml) olive oil

1 Dry-roast dried chilies and shrimp paste separately over low heat until fragrant. 2 Soak dried shrimp in warm water for 10 minutes, then drain. 3 Blend all ingredients to a fine paste in a food processor or blender, adding a little water if necessary. 4 Heat a wok and gently fry paste over moderate heat, stirring frequently, for 10 to 15 minutes or until oil takes on a red color and the mixture is fragrant and thick. 5 Spoon into sterilized jars and seal when cool. Keeps, refrigerated, for 1 month.

*Makes about 2½ cups (600 ml)*

Note: If fresh turmeric is unavailable, increase the ground turmeric measure by 1 tsp.

2½ cups (625 ml) coconut milk

8 tsp. LAKSA PASTE (page 68)

4 tsp. tomato purée

1 tsp. CHILI JAM (page 6)

2½ cups (625 ml) Spiced Vegetable Stock (page 204)

3 tsp. strained lime juice

4 tsp. (20 ml) fish sauce

10 oz. (300 g) Chinese egg noodles

7 oz. (200 g) rice vermicelli (beehoon), soaked until soft

4 fresh tofu squares, deep-fried and cut in half

8 oyster mushrooms, halved

8 snow peas, sliced in half lengthwise

4 tbsp. snow pea sprouts, trimmed

4 oz. (125 g) bean sprouts

3 kaffir lime leaves, shredded

2 hard-boiled eggs, sliced in half lengthwise

4 tsp. cilantro leaves

4 tsp. Vietnamese mint (laksa) leaves

2 small Thai *or* serrano chilies, finely sliced
   into rounds

4 tsp. Fried Shallot Slices (page 201)

4 lime wedges

## Spicy vegetable laksa

**1** Bring coconut milk, LAKSA PASTE, tomato purée, and CHILI JAM slowly to the boil, uncovered, in a saucepan. Reduce heat and simmer for 5 minutes, or until oil rises to surface. **2** Add stock and return to the boil, uncovered. Reduce heat and simmer gently for 10 minutes. Season with lime juice and fish sauce. Taste and, if necessary, adjust seasoning. **3** Scald both types of noodles in boiling water, drain, and divide between 4 bowls. Toss tofu, mushrooms, snow peas, snow pea sprouts, bean sprouts, and lime leaves over noodles. **4** Ladle soup into bowls over vegetables and noodles. Top with sliced egg, cilantro and Vietnamese mint leaves, sliced chilies, and fried shallot slices, and serve with a lime wedge.

*Serves 4*

4 tsp. (20 ml) light soy sauce

1 tsp. sesame oil

½ tsp. freshly ground white pepper

four 5 oz. white fish fillets

2 tbsp. Fried Shallot Slices (page 201)

**Laksa sauce**

4 tsp. (20 ml) vegetable oil

8 tsp. LAKSA PASTE (page 68)

1 stalk lemongrass, roughly chopped

2 small Thai *or* serrano chilies, chopped

2 kaffir lime leaves

¾ cup (200 ml) canned coconut cream

4 tsp. tomato purée

1 cup (250 ml) Fish Stock (page 201)

2 tsp. fish sauce

1 tsp. strained lime juice

## Steamed fish with laksa sauce

**1** To make laksa sauce, heat oil in pan and fry LAKSA PASTE with lemongrass, chilies, and lime leaves for about 5 minutes, or until fragrant. **2** Add coconut cream and tomato purée and bring to simmering point. Cook on gentle heat for 5 minutes, then add stock. Simmer for 20 minutes, then add fish sauce and lime juice. If sauce gets too thick, add a little extra fish stock. Taste and, if necessary, adjust seasoning. **3** Remove from heat and pour sauce through a fine mesh sieve or muslin. Discard solids. Sauce can be made ahead of time and gently reheated when ready to serve. **4** Combine soy sauce, sesame oil, and pepper and brush onto fish fillets. Lay fillets on a plate and place in a steamer tray over gently boiling water. Cover with a lid and steam for 6 to 10 minutes, depending on size and thickness of fish fillets. Test center of fillets with a skewer. Flesh should be white and firm without being dry or breaking open. **5** Place steamed fish on laksa sauce and top with fried shallot slices. Serve with preferred accompaniment – steamed Chinese broccoli (gai lan) or another green leafy vegetable, steamed jasmine rice, roasted tomatoes, or noodles.

*Serves 4*

Note: Any white fish can be used for this dish.

## Stir-fried lemon shrimp and squid

12 green king shrimp
8 small squid, cleaned
3 tbsp. (40 ml) vegetable oil
1 tsp. sesame oil
4 red shallots, finely sliced
2 cloves garlic, finely sliced
2 large red Anaheim *or* Dutch chilies, finely sliced
8 tsp. LAKSA PASTE (page 68)
3 tsp. fish sauce
3½ tbsp. (50 ml) lemon juice
4 oz. (100 g) snow pea sprouts
½ cup lemon basil *or* basil leaves
steamed rice, to serve

**1** Peel and devein shrimp, leaving tails intact. Cut squid tubes into thick strips lengthwise and carefully score inner flesh diagonally. **2** Heat both oils in a wok and fry shallots, garlic, and chilies over high heat for 30 seconds. Add LAKSA PASTE, fish sauce, and lemon juice and fry for another minute or so until fragrant. **3** Add shrimp and squid (tentacles, too, if desired) and toss over high heat for 2 minutes, or until just cooked. Stir to ensure seafood is evenly coated with spice paste. **4** Add snow pea sprouts and toss over heat for another minute. **5** Remove from heat, stir through basil leaves and serve with steamed rice.

*Serves 4*

## Hot-and-sour fish soup

2 tsp. vegetable oil

1 small onion, chopped

8 tsp. LAKSA PASTE (page 68)

6 cups (1.5 l) Fish Stock (page 201) *or* water

¾ cup (200 ml) Tamarind Liquid (page 200)

4 tsp. (20 ml) fish sauce

8 bok choy leaves, shredded

2 tomatoes, peeled and chopped

½ cup (100 g) Chinese long beans, cut into 2 in. (5 cm) lengths (see Note)

2 ears of corn, kernels cut

12 straw mushrooms, cut in half lengthwise

extra vegetable oil, for deep-frying

four 2½ oz. fish fillets

2 cups cooked rice

¼ cup cilantro leaves

**1** Heat oil in a saucepan and fry onion and LAKSA PASTE for a few minutes, or until fragrant. Add stock, tamarind liquid and fish sauce and bring to the boil. Reduce heat and simmer for 10 minutes. **2** Add vegetables and cook for 20 minutes, or until vegetables are very soft. Taste and, if necessary, adjust seasoning. **3** Heat oil in a deep-fryer or saucepan and fry fish fillets for 6 to 8 minutes, or until very crisp. Remove from oil and drain on paper towels. **4** Divide cooked rice between 4 bowls and ladle hot soup over. Top with fried fish and cilantro leaves.

*Serves 4*

Note: Regular green beans can be substituted if Chinese long beans are unavailable.

2 chicken breasts, skin removed
2 cups (500 ml) White Chicken Stock (page 202)
1 cup (250 ml) canned coconut cream
8 tsp. LAKSA PASTE (page 68)
1 tsp. CHILI JAM (page 6)
2 cups (500 ml) coconut milk
2 tsp. strained lime juice
4 tsp. (20 ml) fish sauce
1 lb. (500 g) fresh rice noodles
2 kaffir lime leaves, finely shredded
4 oz. (125 g) bean sprouts
1 small cucumber, peeled, seeded, and shredded
2 tsp. Fried Shallot Slices (page 201)
1 tbsp. cilantro leaves
2 small Thai *or* serrano chilies, finely sliced
16 Vietnamese mint (laksa) leaves

## Coconut chicken laksa

**1** Steam or poach chicken gently in stock for 15 minutes, or until just cooked through. Remove chicken from stock and cool. Shred meat. Reserve stock. **2** Bring coconut cream, LAKSA PASTE, and CHILI JAM slowly to the boil, uncovered, in a saucepan. Reduce heat and simmer for 10 minutes, or until oil rises to surface. **3** Add coconut milk and stock and return to the boil, uncovered. Reduce heat and simmer gently for 15 minutes. Season with lime juice and fish sauce. Taste and, if necessary, adjust seasoning. **4** Put noodles and chicken into separate noodle baskets or conical sieves and lower into soup for about 20 seconds, or until warmed through. **5** Divide noodles and chicken between 4 bowls and add lime leaves and bean sprouts. Ladle soup into each bowl to cover noodles and stir with a chopstick to combine. Sprinkle remaining ingredients over and serve immediately.

*Serves 4*

## Margie's five-minute noodles

1 tsp. LAKSA PASTE (page 68)

1 tsp. CHILI JAM (page 6)

1 tsp. fish sauce

4 tsp. (20 ml) water

1 tsp. sweet soy sauce (kecap manis)

4 oz. (100 g) fresh rice noodle sheets, cut into thick ribbons

handful of tatsoi *or* baby spinach leaves

1½ oz. (50 g) cooked chicken, shredded

2 tsp. Thai basil leaves

2 tsp. cilantro leaves

**1** Mix LAKSA PASTE with CHILI JAM. Heat a wok and dry-fry paste for 1 minute, or until fragrant. **2** Add fish sauce, water, and soy sauce and toss to combine. **3** Add rice noodles and toss over high heat to coat noodles with paste. Cook for 1 minute, or until noodles begin to soften. **4** Add tatsoi, chicken, and basil and continue to toss over high heat for 1 minute, or until chicken is heated through. **5** Remove from heat and add cilantro leaves. Taste and, if necessary, adjust seasoning. Serve immediately.

*Serves 1*

Note: If you are making this dish for more than 1 person, cook each serving separately in a wok for best results.

## Spiced quails with mushrooms

4 small dried Thai chilies, roasted
  and ground
1 tsp. black peppercorns, ground
2 tsp. sea salt
6 large quails, cut in half lengthwise
vegetable oil, for deep-frying
extra 4 tsp. (20 ml) vegetable oil
1 medium onion, finely sliced lengthwise
4 tsp. LAKSA PASTE (page 68)
12 shiitake mushrooms, sliced
12 straw mushrooms, halved lengthwise
2 tbsp. shredded fresh cloud ear fungus (see Note)
2 large red Anaheim *or* Dutch chilies, finely sliced
3 tsp. fish sauce
2 tbsp. (30 ml) sweet soy sauce (kecap manis)
12 green beans, sliced
4 tbsp. torn Thai basil leaves

**1** Combine ground chilies, pepper, and salt and rub into quail halves to season. **2** Heat oil to 350°F (180°C) in a deep-fryer or large pot and deep-fry quail, 6 pieces at a time to maintain oil temperature, for 5 minutes or until crisp and just cooked. Remove from oil and drain on paper towels. Repeat until all quail pieces are cooked. Sprinkle quail with a little of the remaining seasoned salt. **3** Heat extra vegetable oil in a wok and fry onion until softened and beginning to color. Stir in LAKSA PASTE and toss over high heat to combine. **4** Add mushrooms, fungus, and chilies and continue to toss over high heat to combine ingredients thoroughly. **5** Add fish sauce and soy sauce, stir, then toss in beans and cook for another minute. **6** Add basil leaves, taste and, if necessary, adjust seasoning. **7** Place stir-fried mushrooms on plates, lay crisp spiced quails on top and serve immediately.

*Serves 4*

Note: If dried cloud ear fungus is used, soak in hot water first, then proceed as with fresh fungus.

four 5 oz. (150 g) lamb loins *or* backstraps

8 tsp. LAKSA PASTE (page 68)

4 tsp. (20 ml) vegetable oil

2 tbsp. shredded mint leaves

8 stalks lemongrass, trimmed to 4 in. (10 cm) lengths

2 bunches thin asparagus

sea salt

freshly ground black pepper

**Yogurt mint salad**

¼ cup cilantro leaves, shredded

2 tbsp. shredded spearmint leaves

1 small green jalapeño chili, finely sliced into rounds

2 shallots, finely chopped

½ tsp. finely chopped ginger

2 tsp. fish sauce

1 tsp. strained lime juice

¾ cup (200 ml) thick plain yogurt

1 cucumber, peeled, seeded, and cut into julienne

¼ tsp. sea salt

¼ tsp. freshly ground black pepper

# Grilled spiced lamb with mint and asparagus

**1** Trim lamb of any sinew or fat and cut each loin into 8 cubes. **2** Mix LAKSA PASTE, oil, and mint and work into meat. Marinate for 2 hours. Thread 4 lamb cubes onto each lemongrass stalk, keeping the meat pieces close together. **3** Make yogurt mint salad by mixing ingredients thoroughly in a bowl. Keep refrigerated until ready to serve. **4** Heat a cast-iron grill pan or barbecue and grill lamb kebabs for 12 to 15 minutes, or until lamb is tender yet still pink in the center. Remove from heat and rest for a few minutes in a warm place. **5** Trim tough ends from asparagus spears, brush with a little oil, and grill until soft and beginning to scorch. Remove from heat and season to taste. **6** Arrange lamb kebabs and grilled asparagus on plates and serve with yogurt mint salad.

*Serves 4*

# Black Pepper and Lemongrass Stir-fry Paste

Quick and easy stir-frying is so popular these days that you'll want to keep this fragrant and versatile paste in your pantry always. It has a warm, mellow, mid-palate flavor because the black pepper and chili are tempered by the fresh zing of lemongrass and lime, and it responds perfectly to the intense heat of wok cooking by releasing its flavor and aroma immediately. Use it when you stir-fry, to marinate food to be cooked on the barbecue, to spice up a soup, to toss with noodles in a variety of ways (as you will see in this chapter) or to mix with other chili pastes for an even more intense flavor hit.

## Black pepper and lemongrass stir-fry paste

11 oz (350 g) fresh lemongrass stalks
1½ oz. (50 g) shallots, finely chopped
10 tbsp. (150 g) cloves garlic, finely chopped
1½ oz. (50 g) ginger, finely chopped
4 tsp. (20 g) cilantro roots, finely chopped
10 kaffir lime leaves
1½ oz. (50 g) Thai chilies, finely chopped
¼ cup (60 ml) chili oil
4 tsp. (20 g) coarsely ground black pepper
12 large dried Anaheim *or* Dutch chilies,
   dry-roasted and ground
4 tbsp. (50 g) salted black beans
3 tbsp. (40 g) brown sugar (*or* palm sugar, shaved)
3 tbsp. (40 g) Malaysian shrimp paste (belacan),
   dry-roasted
¼ cup (60 ml) light soy sauce
¼ cup (60 ml) fish sauce

**1** Chop lemongrass finely with a knife, to make the paste finer when processed. **2** Blend lemongrass, shallots, garlic, ginger, cilantro root, lime leaves, and fresh chilies with chili oil to a paste in a food processor or blender, then add remaining ingredients. Process paste until it is quite fine. **3** Cook over low heat for 45 minutes. **4** Taste and, if necessary, adjust seasoning. Spoon into sterilized jars, cover with a film of oil, and seal when cool. Keeps, refrigerated, for 1 month.

*Makes about 3 cups (750 ml)*

2 cups cold cooked jasmine rice

3 tbsp. (40 ml) vegetable oil

2 eggs, lightly beaten

1 medium onion, finely sliced lengthwise

4 tsp. BLACK PEPPER AND LEMONGRASS
   STIR-FRY PASTE (page 82)

4 asparagus spears, cut on the diagonal into
   ¾ in. (2 cm) lengths

2 tsp. salted black beans, washed

4 oz. (100 g) bean sprouts

2 tsp. fish sauce

2 tbsp. snipped Chinese chives

2 tbsp. Fried Garlic Slices (page 201)

# Vegetable fried rice

**1** Using a fork, separate rice grains (to ensure even cooking). **2** Heat half the oil in a wok and add beaten egg. Cook until set. Turn egg out of wok, roll up, and slice finely into shreds. Set aside. **3** Heat remaining oil and fry onion with spice paste over high heat for 2 minutes, or until onion begins to color. **4** Add asparagus, black beans, and bean sprouts and toss to combine. **5** Add shredded egg, rice, and fish sauce and stir to combine. Cook over high heat for 1 minute, or until rice is heated through. **6** Remove from heat, sprinkle with chives and fried garlic slices, and serve.

*Serves 4*

## Fried eggplant salad

two 10 oz. (300 g) eggplants

sea salt

vegetable oil, for deep-frying

extra 2 tbsp. (30 ml) vegetable oil

4 tsp. BLACK PEPPER AND LEMONGRASS
   STIR-FRY PASTE (page 82)

5 fresh black wood fungus, shredded (see Note)

2 tbsp. (30 ml) Chinese Shaoxing rice wine

2 tbsp. (30 ml) rice vinegar

3 tbsp. (40 ml) light soy sauce

2 tbsp. (30 ml) White Chicken Stock (page 202) *or* water

2 tsp. fish sauce

2 tsp. sugar

1 tsp. sesame oil

4 scallions, finely sliced into rounds

½ cup cilantro leaves

**1** Quarter eggplants lengthwise, then cut each quarter across into slices 1 in. (2.5 cm) thick. Sprinkle with salt and place on paper towel in a single layer for 30 minutes. **2** Heat vegetable oil in a deep-fryer or large pot to 350°F (180°C). Blot salt and moisture from eggplant slices with paper towels, then deep-fry in small batches until golden. Drain on paper towels. **3** Heat a large wok and add extra vegetable oil. Toss in spice paste and stir-fry quickly. Add fungus and fried eggplant and toss well. Immediately add rice wine, vinegar, soy sauce, stock, fish sauce, and sugar and bring to the boil over high heat. This will take 1 to 2 minutes at most. **4** Reduce heat and simmer for 2 minutes to allow eggplant to absorb some of the liquid. **5** Remove wok from heat and stir in sesame oil, scallions, and cilantro leaves. Serve immediately.

*Serves 4*

Note: If dried black wood fungus is used, soak in hot water first before proceeding as with fresh fungus. A few fresh oyster mushrooms can also be added for texture.

4 large eggs

4 tsp. (20 ml) vegetable oil

4 tsp. BLACK PEPPER AND LEMONGRASS
  STIR-FRY PASTE (page 82)

2 tsp. CHILI JAM (page 6)

1 cup (250 ml) coconut milk

2 tsp. fish sauce

2 tsp. strained lime juice

¼ cup Fried Shallot Slices (page 201)

## Spiced eggs

**1** Put eggs in a saucepan of cold water and bring to the boil, stirring occasionally. Boil for 6 minutes. Remove from heat and plunge into cold water. When cool, peel carefully. **2** Heat oil in a saucepan and cook spice paste with CHILI JAM for 2 to 3 minutes over moderate heat. **3** When paste starts to smell fragrant, stir in coconut milk and bring to a simmer. Add fish sauce and lime juice and simmer for 10 minutes. **4** Add eggs and cook for 15 minutes, or until sauce thickens, stirring regularly to keep eggs coated with sauce. **5** Remove from heat. Taste and, if necessary, adjust seasoning. Spoon eggs and sauce into a serving bowl and sprinkle with fried shallot slices. Serve as part of a multi-dish feast, including rice.

*Serves 4*

12 large green tiger *or* white shrimp
1 tbsp. chopped cilantro leaves
6 tsp. BLACK PEPPER AND LEMONGRASS
   STIR-FRY PASTE (page 82)
twelve 4½ in. (11 cm) square spring roll wrappers
1 egg white
vegetable oil, for deep-frying
Sweet Chili Sauce (page 200) *or* Chinese red vinegar with
   ginger

## Spiced shrimp spring rolls

**1** Peel shrimp, leaving tails intact. Devein, then butterfly shrimp open. **2** Add cilantro leaves to spice paste and brush liberally over prawns. **3** Position 1 prawn on each spring roll wrapper with tail hanging over edge. Roll up securely, tucking edges in as you go. Brush wrapper edges with egg white and seal. **4** Heat vegetable oil in a deep-fryer or large pot to 350°F (180°C). Fry rolls, a few at a time, for 3 minutes or until golden – shrimp should be just cooked. Remove with a slotted spoon and drain on paper towels briefly before serving. **5** Serve with sweet chili sauce or red vinegar with ginger for dipping.

*Serves 4*

vegetable oil, for deep-frying

two 2 lb. (1 kg) mud crabs, cleaned and quartered
  (see Note)

extra ⅓ cup (100 ml) vegetable oil

8 tsp. BLACK PEPPER AND LEMONGRASS
  STIR-FRY PASTE (page 82)

3 tbsp. (40 ml) Chinese oyster sauce

2 tbsp. sliced scallions

## Stir-fried black pepper mud crab

**1** Heat vegetable oil in a deep-fryer or large wok to 350°F (180°C) and fry crab quarters for about 1 minute, or until shells change color. Remove from oil and set aside. **2** In a separate wok, heat extra oil, add spice paste, and stir-fry for 1 minute over high heat to release flavors. **3** Add oyster sauce and crab pieces and toss over heat until crab is well coated. Cook for 3 minutes. Remove from heat, sprinkle with scallions, and serve.

*Serves 4*

Note: Other varieties of crab such as bay, peekytoe, or dungeness can be used if mud crabs are not readily available. Simply adjust the cooking time according to the type and weight of crab you are using.

## Black pepper beef

3 tbsp. (40 ml) Chinese Shaoxing rice wine
4 tsp. (20 ml) fish sauce
8 tsp. BLACK PEPPER AND LEMONGRASS
   STIR-FRY PASTE (page 82)
1 lb. (500 g) beef fillet, cut into ¾ in. (2 cm) cubes
vegetable oil, for deep-frying
2 cloves garlic, finely sliced
2 shallots, finely sliced
3 tbsp. (40 ml) Chinese oyster sauce
4 tsp. (20 ml) light soy sauce
5 oz. (150 g) snow pea shoots
1 tbsp. snipped Chinese chives
1 tsp. Sichuan Spice Salt (page 200)

**1** Mix rice wine with fish sauce and spice paste in a bowl. Add beef and rub in marinade to coat thoroughly and until all moisture has been absorbed by the meat. Cover and leave at room temperature for 30 minutes. **2** Heat oil in a wok and deep-fry beef for 1 minute. Remove with a slotted spoon, drain on paper towel, and set aside. **3** Drain oil from wok, leaving about 1 tbsp. Fry garlic and shallot briefly until they begin to color, then add beef with oyster and soy sauces. Cook over high heat for 1 to 2 minutes, tossing regularly for even cooking. Remove from wok and set aside. **4** In the same hot wok, toss snow pea shoots and chives for a few seconds to wilt and pick up remaining flavors. **5** Arrange greens on serving plates and top with pepper beef. Sprinkle with Sichuan spice salt and serve.

*Serves 4*

Note: This beef is fabulous with Green Bean Sambal (page 45).

four 4 oz. (125 g) white fish fillets (see Note)
4 tsp. BLACK PEPPER AND LEMONGRASS
STIR-FRY PASTE (page 82)
⅔ cup (150 ml) Fish Stock (page 201)
3 tbsp. (40 ml) sweet soy sauce (kecap manis)
4 tsp. (20 ml) fish sauce
½ cup cilantro leaves
steamed rice, to serve

## Steamed spiced fish

**1** Lay fish fillets on a large plate with a lip that will fit into a steamer basket. Mix spice paste with stock, soy sauce, and fish sauce and pour over fish. **2** Place plate in steamer basket, cover with lid, and steam over boiling water for 6 to 8 minutes, depending on thickness and density of fish. Flesh should be opaque when cooked. **3** Remove fish from steamer. Carefully slide onto serving plates and spoon sauce over. Add cilantro leaves and serve with steamed rice.

*Serves 4*

Note: Any of these fish is suitable – grouper, snapper, bream, gurnard, sea bass, perch, coral trout, or pike.

vegetable oil, for deep-frying

4 fresh tofu squares, sliced

4 tsp. (20 ml) chili oil

8 tsp. BLACK PEPPER AND LEMONGRASS
   STIR-FRY PASTE (page 82)

6 macadamia nuts, ground

1⅔ cups (400 ml) White Chicken Stock (page 202)

⅔ cup (150 ml) coconut milk

½ cup (100 g) sweet potato, cooked and puréed

2 chicken breasts, finely sliced

13 oz. (400 g) fresh Chinese egg noodles, blanched
   (see Note)

3 cups (150 g) bean sprouts

4 scallions, finely sliced

1 small cucumber, chopped

1 large green chili, seeded and finely sliced

½ cup chopped Chinese celery (kun choy) *or* plain celery

3 tsp. fish sauce

¼ cup cilantro leaves

4 tsp. Fried Shallot Slices (page 201)

1 lime, quartered

## Spicy chicken noodles with tofu

**1** Heat vegetable oil in a wok and fry tofu, a few slices at a time, over high heat, turning carefully with a mesh spoon until golden and puffed. Remove carefully and drain on paper towels. Discard oil. **2** Heat chili oil in wok and fry spice paste and ground macadamia nuts over low heat until fragrant. Add stock, coconut milk, and sweet potato purée and bring to the boil. The purée will thicken the sauce as it cooks. **3** Reduce heat, stir in chicken, and cook for 2 minutes. Add noodles, bean sprouts, scallions, cucumber, chili, and celery and cook for 2 minutes, or until warmed through. Add fish sauce. Taste and, if necessary, adjust seasoning. **4** Ladle into deep bowls and top with fried tofu, cilantro leaves, fried shallots, and lime wedges.
*Serves 4*

Note: Dried Chinese egg noodles may be substituted, and should be blanched before use.

# Satay Spice Paste

Typical of Malay Nonya and Indonesian cooking, this paste is used as a marinade and flavor booster for meat, poultry or seafood, which can then be threaded on satay sticks and barbecued or grilled. The flavors are redolent of the street carts whose vendors ply these delicacies throughout much of Southeast Asia. As a snack, satay has universal appeal. For best results cook over glowing charcoal embers. Satay spice paste can just as easily be used in other quick-cooking applications such as stir-frying, deep-frying or pan-frying.

1 tsp. fennel seeds

1 tsp. cumin seeds

2 tsp. coriander seeds

½ tsp. black peppercorns

1 tbsp. (30 g) brown sugar (*or* palm sugar, shaved)

¾ cup (200 ml) coconut milk

2 tsp. ground turmeric

½ tsp. chili powder

1 tsp. finely chopped lime zest

2 tsp. sea salt

## Satay spice paste

**1** Dry-roast whole spices separately over gentle heat until fragrant. Cool, then grind to a fine powder. **2** Stir brown sugar into coconut milk over gentle heat until it has dissolved, then mix in all spices and flavorings. Keeps, refrigerated, for up to 48 hours.

*Makes about 1¼ cups (300 ml)*

2 tsp. finely chopped garlic

8 tsp. SATAY SPICE PASTE (page 96)

2 tsp. sea salt

1 cup (150 g) chickpea flour (besan)

1 tsp. baking powder

½ cup (125 ml) water

vegetable oil, for deep-frying

2 cups diced *or* chopped mixed vegetables (cauliflower,
    broccoli, potato, peas, carrot, zucchini, eggplant)

## Spicy vegetable fritters

**1** To make batter, combine garlic, SATAY SPICE PASTE, and salt in a food processor. Blend in flour and baking powder, then add water and mix to a smooth batter. Refrigerate for 2 hours before using. The batter should have reasonable body without being too thick. If it looks too thick, add a little water. **2** Heat vegetable oil to 350°F (180°C) in a deep-fryer or large pot. **3** Add chopped vegetables to batter. Drop spoonfuls of battered vegetables, a few at a time, into hot oil and fry for 4 minutes, or until golden and crisp. Remove fritters from oil with a slotted spoon, drain on paper towels, and keep warm. Repeat process until all batter has been used. Serve with a yogurt-based dip or raita.

*Serves 4*

1 lb. (500 g) cleaned squid bodies (see Note)
4 tsp. SATAY SPICE PASTE (page 96)
3 cloves garlic, finely chopped
1 tsp. ground turmeric
4 tsp. (20 ml) vegetable oil
4 tsp. (20 ml) Tamarind Liquid (page 200)
2 tsp. sweet soy sauce (kecap manis)

## Stir-fried turmeric squid

1 Split squid bodies in half lengthwise and cut into strips 1 in. (2.5 cm) wide. Carefully score inner flesh diagonally. 2 Mix SATAY SPICE PASTE with garlic and turmeric and marinate squid in this for 30 minutes. 3 Heat oil in a wok or cast-iron pan and fry squid over high heat for 1 minute, or until it begins to curl. 4 Add tamarind liquid and sweet soy sauce and toss over heat to combine. Cook for another minute and remove from heat. Serve immediately as a snack or as part of a selection of dishes.

*Serves 4*

Note: If you clean your own squid, don't discard the tentacles – add them to the marinade.

## Vegetable curry puffs

2 large potatoes, peeled and diced
2 sweet potatoes, peeled and diced
3 tbsp. (40 ml) vegetable oil
1 medium onion, finely diced
3 cloves garlic, minced
2 tsp. minced ginger
8 tsp. SATAY SPICE PASTE (page 96)
¼ cup peas
½ tsp. sea salt
½ tsp. freshly ground black pepper
extra vegetable oil, for deep-frying
**Pastry**
1 lb. (500 g) all-purpose flour
1 tsp. sea salt
4 tbsp. (50 g) lard
7 tbsp. (100 g) unsalted butter
¾ cup (200 ml) water

**1** To make the pastry, mix flour and salt, then, using your hands, work lard and butter into flour until mixture resembles dry crumbs. Add water and continue to mix until dough forms. Wrap in plastic wrap and set aside for 1 hour. **2** Cook potato and sweet potato in lightly salted boiling water for a few minutes until softened. Remove from heat, drain, and refresh in cold water to stop cooking process. Drain again and set aside until ready to use. **3** Heat oil in a frying pan and sauté onion, garlic, and ginger until starting to color. Stir in SATAY SPICE PASTE and cook for 2 minutes. Stir in potato, sweet potatoes, and peas. Simmer gently for 2 minutes. Remove from heat and season to taste. Allow mixture to cool thoroughly before assembling pastries. **4** Roll pastry to a thickness of about ¼ in. (5 mm). Cut into 3 in. (8 cm) circles. Put 1 tbsp. vegetable mixture into center of each circle and fold pastry over to make a half-circle. Press edges and crimp together to secure. **5** Heat oil to 350°F (180°C) in a deep-fryer or large pot. Fry a few curry puffs at a time (to maintain oil temperature) for 5 minutes or until golden. Drain on paper towels. Continue until all pastries have been cooked. Serve hot with a yogurt-based dipping sauce or relish.

*Makes 20*

1¾ cups (400 ml) coconut milk
8 tsp. SATAY SPICE PASTE (page 96)
2 kaffir lime leaves
1 Thai chili, split lengthwise
4 tsp. (20 ml) Tamarind Liquid (page 200)
4 tsp. (20 ml) fish sauce
8 hard-boiled duck eggs (see Note)
½ cup cilantro leaves
2 tbsp. Fried Shallot Slices (page 201)

# Fragrant duck eggs

**1** Bring coconut milk to boiling point and stir in SATAY SPICE PASTE, lime leaves, and chili. Simmer gently for 5 minutes until sauce thickens. **2** Reduce heat to a low simmer and add tamarind liquid, fish sauce, and duck eggs. Simmer gently for 6 to 8 minutes until eggs are heated through and well coated with sauce. **3** Spoon eggs and sauce into a bowl and sprinkle with cilantro leaves and fried shallot slices. Serve with crisp roti or naan bread, parathas, or pappadams.

*Serves 4*

Note: Chicken eggs can be substituted for the duck eggs. This dish can also be served as part of a large communal feast.

## Satay shrimp with green papaya salad

24 green king shrimp

8 tsp. SATAY SPICE PASTE (page 96)

**Green papaya salad**

2 tbsp. (30 ml) strained lime juice

2 tsp. Tamarind Liquid (page 200)

4 tsp. (20 ml) Sugar Syrup (page 201) *or*
 3 tsp. sugar

4 tsp. (20 ml) fish sauce

1 cup (250 g) green papaya, finely shredded

1 tbsp. dried shrimp, ground

6 cherry tomatoes, quartered

1 tbsp. shallot slices

2 Thai *or* serrano chilies, finely sliced

1 tbsp. shredded basil leaves

2 tbsp. raw peanuts, lightly roasted and
 roughly chopped

**1** Soak 12 wooden skewers in water for 1 hour (to prevent them from burning during cooking). Peel and devein shrimp, leaving their tails intact, and marinate in SATAY SPICE PASTE for 30 minutes. **2** Thread 2 shrimp onto each satay stick. **3** To make papaya salad, mix lime juice, tamarind liquid, sugar syrup, and fish sauce together. Combine remaining ingredients in a bowl, keeping aside 2 tsp. chopped peanuts, and toss with dressing. **4** Cook shrimp over charcoal on a barbecue or on or under a grill for about 3 to 4 minutes only, or until just cooked. Remove skewers and serve shrimp on papaya salad, sprinkled with remaining nuts.

*Serves 4*

13 oz. (400 g) chicken breasts, cut into thin
strips 1 in. (2.5 cm) long
8 tsp. SATAY SPICE PASTE (page 96)
4 tbsp. Peanut Chili Sauce (page 7)

## Satay chicken with peanut chili sauce

**1** Soak wooden skewers in water for 1 hour (to prevent them from burning during cooking). Marinate chicken in SATAY SPICE PASTE for 30 minutes to 1 hour. **2** Thread 3 pieces of chicken onto each skewer, keeping pieces close together to maintain moisture during cooking. Cook on a hot cast-iron grill pan or barbecue or under a grill for 5 to 6 minutes, turning for even cooking. The meat will become firm when cooked, but cooking time will depend on the thickness of the pieces. **3** Meanwhile, heat peanut chili sauce in a saucepan. **4** Serve satay chicken with sauce.

*Serves 4*

3 tbsp. (40 ml) vegetable oil
8 shallots
8 tsp. SATAY SPICE PASTE (page 96)
4 tsp. hot curry powder
2 tsp. CHILI JAM (page 6)
2 lb. (1 kg) beef rump *or* topside, cut into ¾ in. (2 cm)
   cubes
2 ripe tomatoes, peeled and chopped
1 stalk lemongrass, cut in half
1⅔ cups (400 ml) thick plain yogurt
¾ cup (200 ml) heavy cream
4 tsp. (20 ml) fish sauce
2 tsp. strained lime juice
steamed basmati rice, to serve

# Spiced beef korma

**1** Preheat oven to low at 300°F (150°C). Heat oil in a large ovenproof wok or pot and fry shallots with SATAY SPICE PASTE, curry powder, and CHILI JAM, stirring often to prevent burning, for 2 to 3 minutes or until fragrant. **2** Add beef and stir to coat thoroughly with spice paste. Cook for 5 minutes to brown meat. **3** Add tomato, lemongrass, yogurt and cream and bring to simmering point over gentle heat. **4** Cover pot with a lid and cook in oven for 25 minutes. Check pot – if korma appears dry, add a little water to keep it moist. Return pot to oven for 20 minutes, or until sauce has been completely absorbed by meat. **5** Remove pot from oven. Discard lemongrass stalks and season korma with fish sauce and lime juice. The curry should have a characteristic rich, oily finish. Serve with steamed basmati rice.

*Serves 4*

# Spiced Tomato Chili Pickle

This relish is of south Indian origin and is known on the subcontinent as tomato kasaundi. It is traditionally served as a condiment with breads and fish dishes, but you will find its flavor extremely versatile and easily adaptable to a variety of uses, not restricted to Indian-style preparations. It has a characteristic sweet–sour, spicy flavor with the chili component being very mild on the palate, much like pepper. Serve it simply as a dipping sauce with vegetable antipasto or fried savory pastries, or stir it into lentils or through noodles or pasta.

## Spiced tomato chili pickle

4 tsp. brown *or* Chinese mustard seeds

½ cup (125 ml) cider vinegar

8 tsp. cumin seeds

½ cup (125 ml) vegetable oil

pinch of freshly ground cloves

2 tsp. ground turmeric

8 tsp. finely chopped ginger

10 cloves garlic

10 small Thai chilies

4½ lb. (2 kg) ripe tomatoes, peeled and quartered

⅓ cup (75 g) brown sugar (*or* palm sugar, shaved)

¼ cup (60 ml) fish sauce

**1** Cook mustard seeds in vinegar over moderate heat for 10 minutes, then set aside for 2 hours. **2** Dry-roast cumin seeds over gentle heat until fragrant. Cool, then grind to a fine powder. **3** Heat oil in a heavy-bottomed pan and fry ground cumin, cloves, and turmeric gently until fragrant. Remove from heat. **4** Process mustard seed mixture, ginger, garlic, and chilies in an electric blender until smooth and add to oil and spices. Add tomato and cook over low heat, stirring frequently, for 1 hour, or until tomato has broken down and sauce is quite smooth. **5** Add brown sugar and fish sauce and cook for a further 30 minutes. Taste and, if necessary, adjust seasoning. **6** Spoon into sterilized jars, cover with a film of oil, and seal when cool. Keeps, refrigerated, for 1 month.

*Makes about 2 cups (500 ml)*

12 tomatoes, cut in half lengthwise
4 tbsp. (50 g) ghee
2 medium onions, chopped
6 cloves garlic, finely chopped
2 tsp. chopped ginger
2 Thai *or* serrano chilies, finely chopped
seeds from 8 green cardamom pods, ground
1 tsp. Garam Masala (page 200)
8 tsp. SPICED TOMATO CHILI PICKLE (page 108)
2 cups (500 ml) Brown Chicken Stock (page 202)
1 tsp. sea salt
1 tsp. freshly ground black pepper

## Tomato-cardamom sauce

**1** Preheat oven to moderately hot at 400°F (200°C) and roast tomatoes on a sheet pan for 25 minutes. Cool. Pass through a conical sieve or food mill, pressing to extract as much juice and pulp as possible. Discard seeds and skin. **2** Melt ghee in a wide, heavy-bottomed saucepan and fry onion, garlic, ginger, and chili until fragrant and softened. Add cardamom and garam masala and fry, stirring, for a few minutes, or until fragrant. **3** Add reserved tomato pulp and SPICED TOMATO CHILI PICKLE and cook over high heat until bubbling. Lower heat and simmer for 10 minutes, or until slightly reduced. **4** Add stock and continue to simmer for 20 minutes. Season with salt and pepper. Cool, skimming surface when necessary. Reheat gently as required and serve with grilled fish or roasted poultry or meat.

*Makes about 2½ cups (600 ml)*

vegetable oil, for deep-frying

8 asparagus spears, trimmed to 2 in. (5 cm) lengths

8 lengthwise slices zucchini

1 green bell pepper, cut into eighths lengthwise
   and seeded

4 scallions, cut into 2 in. (5 cm) lengths

all-purpose flour

Tempura Batter (page 201)

8 basil leaves

8 large mint leaves

4 sprigs of flat-leaf parsley

4 tbsp. SPICED TOMATO CHILI PICKLE (page 108)

## Green vegetable tempura with spiced tomato chili pickle

**1** Heat oil in a deep-fryer or large pot to 350°F (180°C). Dust vegetables and herbs with flour, then dip into tempura batter. **2** Deep-fry vegetables and herbs in hot oil, a few pieces at a time, for 1 minute. Remove with a slotted spoon and drain on paper towels. **3** Pile vegetable tempura on a large plate and serve with SPICED TOMATO CHILI PICKLE as a condiment.

*Serves 4*

## Spaghetti with crabmeat, pimiento, and spiced tomato chili pickle

½ lb. (250 g) spaghetti

¼ cup (50 ml) extra-virgin olive oil

4 tsp. Saffron Butter (page 200)

1 small red onion, finely chopped

6 cloves garlic, finely chopped

2 small Thai *or* serrano chilies, finely chopped

2 tomatoes, peeled, seeded and finely chopped

8 tsp. SPICED TOMATO CHILI PICKLE (page 108)

2½ oz. (75 g) roasted strips pimiento (Spanish piquillo) pepper

1 lb. (500 g) cooked crabmeat (blue, bay, peekytoe *or* dungeness)

½ cup shaved fennel bulb

1 tsp. sea salt

1 tsp. freshly ground black pepper

¼ cup torn basil leaves

**1** Cook spaghetti in a large pot of lightly salted boiling water. **2** Meanwhile, heat oil and saffron butter in a heavy-bottomed frying pan. Add onion, garlic, and chili and cook gently for 1 minute until fragrant, but not colored. **3** Add tomato, SPICED TOMATO CHILI PICKLE, and pimiento strips and cook until simmering. **4** Add crabmeat and fennel and toss over heat to combine. Season with salt and pepper. **5** Drain pasta and toss with a little extra oil. Add crab sauce and basil and toss to coat pasta. Ladle pasta into bowls to serve.

*Serves 4*

four ¼ lb. (125 g) salmon fillets, with skin
extra-virgin olive oil
½ tsp. sea salt
½ tsp. freshly ground black pepper
**Spiced red pepper sauce**
3 red bell peppers
3 tbsp. (40 ml) olive oil
1 large onion, diced
3 cloves garlic, finely diced
2 small Thai *or* serrano chilies, chopped
sea salt, to taste
freshly ground black pepper, to taste
8 tsp. SPICED TOMATO CHILI PICKLE (page 108)
½ cup (100 ml) heavy cream

## Seared salmon with spiced red pepper sauce

**1** To make sauce, preheat oven to moderately hot at 400°F (200°C). Rub peppers with a little oil and roast on a sheet pan for 30 minutes, or until they are blistered and blackened on the surface. Remove from heat and cool slightly. Remove skins, stalk ends, and seeds. **2** Heat remaining oil in a frying pan and cook onion, garlic, and chili until soft and golden. Remove from heat. **3** Process roasted peppers with onion mixture in an electric blender or food processor until smooth. Pass through a conical sieve or food mill, pressing as hard as possible to extract as much juice and pulp as possible. Discard solids and season to taste. Reheat sauce to simmering point in a pan with SPICED TOMATO CHILI PICKLE and cream. **4** To cook fish, preheat oven to moderate at 350°F (180°C). Heat an ovenproof frying pan, add a little oil, and add salmon fillets, skin-side down. Sprinkle with salt and pepper and fry over moderately high heat for 2 minutes, or until juices are sealed in and skin is crisp. Place pan in oven for 4 minutes. Remove fish from oven and carefully slide fillets onto warmed plates. Serve with spiced red pepper sauce.

*Serves 4*

2 bunches spinach, stems removed

4 tbsp. SPICED TOMATO CHILI PICKLE (page 108)

8 tsp. Saffron Butter (page 200)

16 fresh, plump sea scallops

¼ cup cilantro leaves

2 tbsp. shredded mint leaves

2 ripe medium tomatoes, peeled, seeded, and diced

½ tsp. sea salt

½ tsp. freshly ground black pepper

2 tbsp. (30 g) unsalted butter

8 spearmint leaves, shredded

## Saffron scallops with spiced tomato sauce

**1** Wash spinach thoroughly. Blanch in boiling water for 30 seconds and refresh immediately in ice water. When cold, squeeze out water. **2** Bring SPICED TOMATO CHILI PICKLE to a simmer in a saucepan over moderate heat. Stir in saffron butter and scallops and cook, stirring regularly, over gentle heat for 3 minutes. Remove from heat and stir in cilantro, mint, and tomato and season with salt and pepper. **3** Melt butter in a saucepan, add spinach and reheat gently, stirring. Season to taste. Divide spinach between four plates, top with spiced scallops, spoon sauce around, and garnish with shredded spearmint leaves. Serve immediately.

*Serves 4*

Note: If your scallops are particularly large, this recipe will serve 8 people as a "taster." Serve 1 scallop per person, as in the photograph opposite.

## Salt-baked barramundi with spiced tomato chili sauce

4 lb. (2 kg) rock salt

1 whole 4½ lb. (2 kg) wild *or* sea-farmed barramundi, cleaned and scaled (see Note)

4 quarters PRESERVED LEMON (page 124)

1 bunch dill

½ tsp. sea salt

1 tsp. freshly ground black pepper

4 tbsp. SPICED TOMATO CHILI PICKLE (page 108)

3 tbsp. (50 g) unsalted butter

2 tsp. lemon juice

**1** Preheat oven to hot at 450°F (220°C). Lay half the rock salt in the base of a roasting pan large enough to hold the fish. **2** Chop PRESERVED LEMON and place inside fish cavity with dill. Season fish cavity with sea salt and pepper. **3** Lay fish on salt base and cover with remaining rock salt, leaving tail out. Cover tail with foil. Bake for 15 minutes (less for smaller fish), then test with a skewer to see if the fish is warm right through. It may require a further 5 minutes or so, but be careful not to overcook it or fish will dry out. **4** Remove fish from heat and rest for 5 minutes. Scrape off rock salt and skin before fish cools. **5** Heat SPICED TOMATO CHILI PICKLE to simmering point with butter and lemon juice. Carefully lift fish out of pan and discard lemon filling. Portion fish evenly and serve with sauce.

*Serves 8*

Note: Fish such as halibut, Chilean sea bass, or snapper can be substituted for barramundi.

four 5 oz. (150 g) yellowfin tuna steaks (see Note)

4 tsp. (20 ml) olive oil

1 tsp. freshly ground black pepper

½ tsp. cayenne pepper

½ tsp. sea salt

**Tomato and pepper salsa**

4 ripe tomatoes, peeled, seeded, and finely diced

2 red bell peppers, roasted and finely diced

2 yellow bell peppers, roasted and finely diced

1 small red onion, finely diced

4 tsp. SPICED TOMATO CHILI PICKLE (page 108)

½ cup flat-leaf parsley leaves, shredded

2 tbsp. small capers, washed

½ cup (125 ml) extra-virgin olive oil

## Grilled tuna steaks with tomato and pepper salsa

**1** To make the salsa, combine all ingredients. Set aside until ready to serve. **2** Brush each tuna steak with oil and season with pepper and cayenne. Grill or barbecue steaks on medium-high heat for 3 minutes. Turn steaks and cook for an extra minute, leaving them quite rare in the center to retain maximum moisture. Remove from heat and sprinkle with sea salt. **3** Serve with tomato and pepper salsa and a salad of green leaves or arugula.

*Serves 4*

Note: Swordfish, marlin, dolphin fish, or Chilean sea bass can be substituted for tuna.

4 tsp. Caramelized Onion (page 201)

four 3 in. (7.5 cm) shortcrust tart shells, baked blind

5 oz. (150 g) fresh goat's cheese, slightly crumbled

1 tbsp. roasted strips pimiento (Spanish piquillo) pepper, finely sliced

1 egg

1 tbsp. crème fraîche

½ tsp. sea salt

¼ tsp. freshly ground black pepper

1 tbsp. flat-leaf parsley, shredded

3 tbsp. SPICED TOMATO CHILI PICKLE (page 108)

## Baked goat's cheese and pimiento tarts with spiced tomato chili pickle

**1** Preheat oven to moderate at 350°F (180°C). **2** Spread 1 tsp. caramelized onion on base of each tart shell. Pile goat's cheese on top and arrange some pimiento strips around the cheese. **3** Mix egg and crème fraîche and season with salt and pepper. Spoon into tart shells until full. **4** Bake tarts for 10 minutes, or until just set. (Cooking time will vary if different sized tart shells are used.) Remove from oven and sprinkle with parsley. Serve with warmed SPICED TOMATO CHILI PICKLE.

*Makes 4*

## Lamb's brain fritters with tomato-cardamom sauce

4 sets lamb's brains
1 tbsp. all-purpose flour
2 eggs, beaten
sea salt
freshly ground white pepper
2 tbsp. fine breadcrumbs
½ cup (125 ml) Tomato-cardamom Sauce (page 109)
2 tbsp. diced tomato
2 tbsp. shredded flat-leaf parsley
vegetable oil, for deep-frying
2 oz. (60 g) arugula leaves

**1** Poach lamb's brains in simmering water for 2 minutes. Remove from heat and plunge into ice-cold water to stop cooking. **2** Separate lobes and peel brains, discarding membrane. Slice each lobe in half lengthwise. Dust pieces in flour, then dip in beaten egg and coat with seasoned breadcrumbs. Rest on paper towels until ready to cook. **3** Heat tomato-cardamom sauce gently. Stir in tomato and parsley. **4** Heat oil in a deep-fryer or large pot to 350°F (180°C) and fry brains, a few pieces at a time (to maintain oil temperature), for 2 minutes. Remove with a slotted spoon and drain on paper towels. **5** Sit arugula leaves on plates and arrange brain fritters on top. Spoon tomato-cardamom sauce over and serve.

*Serves 4*

twelve 4½ in. (11 cm) square spring roll wrappers
1 egg white
vegetable oil, for deep-frying
4 tbsp. SPICED TOMATO CHILI PICKLE (page 108)
**Beef stuffing**
4 tsp. (20 ml) vegetable oil
1 medium onion, finely chopped
3 cloves garlic, finely chopped
1 tbsp. mild curry powder
2 tsp. CHILI JAM (page 6)
6 oz. (185 g) ground beef
4 oz. (125 g) potatoes, boiled and finely diced
2 tbsp. cilantro leaves
½ tsp. sea salt
½ tsp. freshly ground black pepper

## Beef and potato pastries with spiced tomato chili pickle

**1** To make beef stuffing, heat oil and fry onion and garlic until lightly colored. Add curry powder and fry for about 2 minutes. Stir in CHILI JAM and ground beef and cook over moderate heat for 5 minutes, or until meat is just cooked through. Remove from heat and cool. Mix potato and cilantro into cooled meat mixture and season. Allow stuffing to cool completely before assembling pastries. **2** Lay a spring roll wrapper on a board and place some beef stuffing in center. Fold pastry over and fold in edges to seal into a log shape. Brush open edge with egg white and roll over to seal. **3** Heat oil in a deep-fryer or large pot to 350°F (180°C) and deep-fry the pastries, a few at a time (to maintain oil temperature), for 2 minutes or until golden. Remove with a slotted spoon and drain on paper towels. **4** Serve with SPICED TOMATO CHILI PICKLE as a dipping sauce.

*Makes 12*

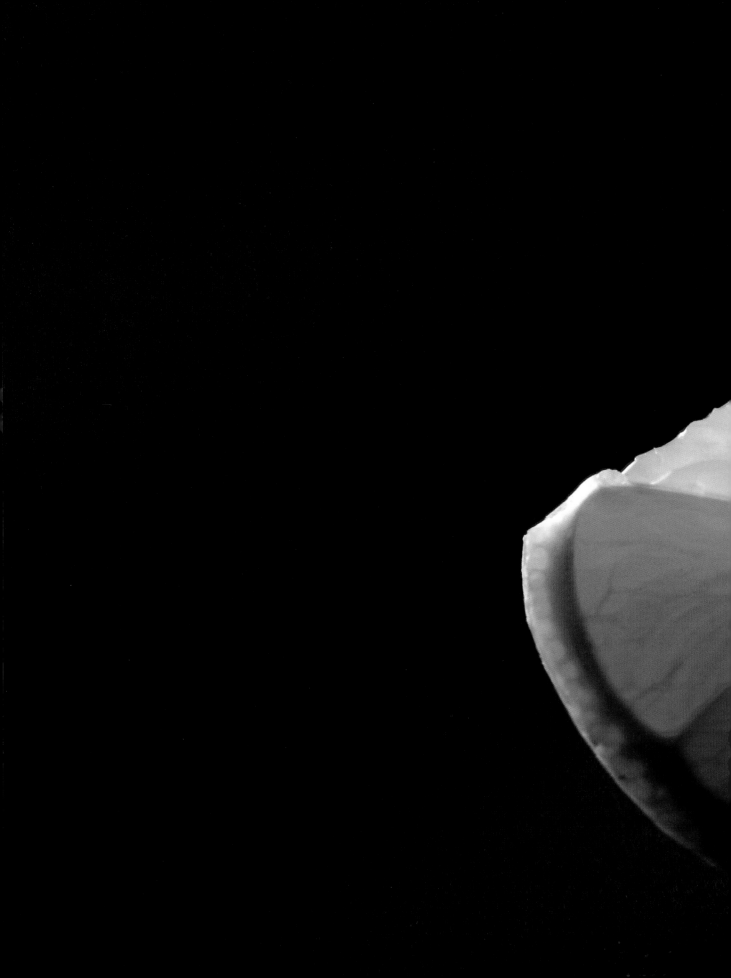

# Preserved Lemons

Lemons are an essential element in many cooking processes. A natural agent of change, their acidity brings balance and harmony to food. Lemons enhance flavors and, when preserved, give them an incomparable complexity. Fresh lemon zest or its juice is no substitute for the smooth mellow character of a preserved lemon. Often used in conjunction with aromatic spices and herbs, preserved lemons provide a foil to the richness of meat and the oiliness of fish and olives, while at the same time transforming an "acceptable" dish into a taste sensation.

8 ripe lemons
1 cup (250 g) fine table salt
lemon juice, to cover

Preserved lemons

**1** Wash lemons thoroughly, scrubbing skins if necessary. Cut into quarters lengthwise to within ½ in. (1 cm) of base. Pack each piece with salt and reshape fruit by pressing back together. **2** Put lemons into a sterilized 2 qt. (2 l) preserving jar and sprinkle with a little extra salt. Cover with lemon juice. Seal and store for 6 weeks in a cool place away from direct light. **3** When lemons are ready to use, remove from jar as needed and rinse with water before proceeding. Discard flesh and use only the zest in any of the preparations given here. If stored in a cool place away from light, PRESERVED LEMONS will keep for 6 months.

2 ripe avocados, chopped
1 clove garlic, finely chopped
1 tsp. CHILI JAM (page 6)
½ tsp. sea salt
¼ tsp. freshly ground black pepper
2 tsp. lemon juice
8 cherry tomatoes, quartered
zest of 1 PRESERVED LEMON (page 124),
   finely diced
2 tbsp. chopped cilantro leaves

## Preserved lemon guacamole

**1** In a food processor, blend avocado with garlic, CHILI JAM, salt, pepper, and lemon juice until smooth.
**2** Spoon into a bowl and stir through the tomato, PRESERVED LEMON zest, and coriander. Serve as a dip with crusty bread, wafers, or corn chips or as an accompaniment to grilled fish or barbecued poultry.

*Serves 4*

1 lb. (500 g) kalamata olives

2 tsp. cumin seeds, roasted

zest of 1 PRESERVED LEMON (page 124),
   cut into strips

2 small Thai *or* serrano chilies, finely sliced

2 cloves garlic

2 sprigs of thyme *or* flat-leaf parsley, shredded

1 tsp. black peppercorns

1 cup (250 ml) extra-virgin olive oil

## Spiced black olives with preserved lemon

**1** Place all ingredients in a clean jar and cover with oil. **2** Remove from oil as required and serve with drinks or use to flavor pasta or a feta cheese salad.

## Chermoula with preserved lemon

1 tsp. cumin seeds

10 shallots, finely sliced

4 large cloves garlic, finely chopped

¼ cup flat-leaf parsley, finely chopped

½ cup cilantro leaves,
    finely chopped

½ cup spearmint leaves, finely chopped

2 Thai chilies, finely chopped

½ tsp. freshly ground black pepper

zest of ½ PRESERVED LEMON (page 124),
    diced

¾ cup (200 ml) extra-virgin olive oil

1 Mix all ingredients thoroughly. 2 Spoon into a jar and cover with a film of oil. Keeps, refrigerated, for up to 3 days. Use when cooking fish or chicken, or toss with boiled potatoes.

*Makes about 1¹/₂ cups (350 ml)*

7 oz. (200 g) fresh tuna (canned tuna may be
  substituted)
½ tsp. freshly ground black pepper
¾ cup (200 ml) extra-virgin olive oil
sea salt
½ lb. (250 g) spaghetti
½ fennel bulb, finely shaved
1 tbsp. finely chopped garlic
3 tbsp. (40 ml) lemon juice
3 tbsp. shredded flat-leaf parsley
1 tbsp. small capers, washed
1 tbsp. finely sliced *or* chopped zest of PRESERVED
  LEMON (page 124)

## Spaghetti with tuna, preserved lemon, capers, and fennel

**1** Sprinkle tuna lightly with pepper. Heat a little of the oil in a frying pan and sear tuna on both sides over high heat for 2 minutes. Remove from heat and allow to cool briefly, then slice finely. **2** Heat a large pot of water to boiling point, add a pinch of salt, and cook spaghetti until al dente. Drain immediately. **3** Meanwhile, combine remaining oil, tuna, fennel, garlic, lemon juice, parsley, capers, and PRESERVED LEMON zest in a large bowl. Season to taste with salt and pepper. **4** Toss pasta through tuna mixture and serve immediately.

*Serves 4*

⅔ cup (150 ml) Chermoula with Preserved Lemon
    (page 128)
four ¼ lb. (125 g) salmon fillets, taken from thickest
    part of fish (see Note)
2 bunches spinach, stalks removed
4 tbsp. (50 g) unsalted butter
½ tsp. sea salt
½ tsp. freshly ground black pepper
pinch of freshly grated nutmeg
4 tsp. extra-virgin olive oil

# Baked salmon with preserved lemon chermoula

**1** Prepare 4 sheets of parchment paper and 4 sheets of foil, each 8 in. (20 cm) square. On each piece of parchment paper, spread 4 tsp. chermoula and lay a salmon fillet on top. Spread another 4 tsp. chermoula on top of each fillet. Fold paper over to make secure packages, then wrap each in foil. Allow salmon to marinate for 30 minutes at room temperature before cooking. Preheat oven to moderately hot at 400°F (200°C). **2** Wash spinach leaves thoroughly, blanch in boiling water for 30 seconds, and refresh immediately in ice water to stop cooking process and retain green color. Squeeze out excess water and set aside until ready to use. **3** Bake salmon parcels on a sheet pan for 8 to 10 minutes, depending on thickness of fillets. The fish should have a rosy blush in the middle to retain maximum moisture. **4** While fish is baking, heat a frying pan and melt butter over low heat. Add spinach, salt, pepper, and nutmeg. Stir continually over medium heat for about 4 minutes, or until spinach has softened and is warmed through. **5** When fish is cooked, remove parcels from oven and unwrap. Spoon spinach onto 4 plates and slide fish on top. Pour over any juices from the packets and drizzle each serving with 1 tsp. olive oil.

*Serves 4*

Note: For variety, substitute ocean trout, freshwater salmon, Arctic char, halibut, or Chilean sea bass for the salmon.

## Rice pilaf with raisins, pine nuts, preserved lemon, and herbs

5 tbsp. (75 g) ghee

1 medium onion, finely chopped

2 cloves garlic, finely chopped

1 stick of cinnamon

1¼ cups (200 g) basmati rice

¼ cup (40 g) pine nuts, lightly roasted

¼ cup (40 g) raisins

2 cups (500 ml) water

2 tsp. chopped chervil

1 tsp. chopped mint leaves

2 tsp. chopped flat-leaf parsley

1 tsp. chopped cilantro leaves

4 tsp. diced zest of PRESERVED LEMON (page 124)

1 tsp. sea salt

1 tsp. freshly ground black pepper

**1** Heat ghee in a large pan and cook onion and garlic over moderate heat for about 3 minutes, or until softened. **2** Add cinnamon stick and rice and stir to coat with onion mixture. Add pine nuts, raisins, and water. **3** Cover pan with a lid, reduce heat to low, and simmer for 15 to 20 minutes, or until liquid has been absorbed and rice is cooked. Remove cinnamon stick and discard. **4** Remove pan from heat and stir in chopped herbs and PRESERVED LEMON zest. Season with salt and pepper. Serve with fried fish, steamed chicken, grilled lamb, or roast beef.

*Serves 4*

½ lb. (250 g) tagliatelle *or* other pasta
¼ lb. (125 g) feta cheese, slightly crumbled (see Note)
¾ cup (200 g) cherry tomatoes, halved and lightly roasted
zest of 1 PRESERVED LEMON (page 124), diced
1 tbsp. shredded flat-leaf parsley
12 basil leaves, shredded
⅓ cup (100 ml) extra-virgin olive oil
8 cloves garlic, roasted
1 tsp. sea salt
1 tsp. freshly ground black pepper
4 tsp. freshly grated parmesan cheese

## Feta, preserved lemon, and tomato pasta

**1** Cook pasta in salted boiling water until al dente. Drain. **2** Combine remaining ingredients, except parmesan, in a bowl, add hot pasta, and toss to mix well. Sprinkle with parmesan and serve immediately.

*Serves 4*

Note: Ricotta or fresh goat's cheese can be used in place of feta cheese.

## Saffron tomato soup with grilled rouget fillet and shrimp

12 ripe tomatoes
½ cup (125 ml) extra-virgin olive oil
1 small onion, finely chopped
4 cloves garlic, finely chopped
2 tsp. diced fennel bulb
1 Thai chili, finely chopped
1 small leek, finely diced
1 tbsp. diced carrot
½ tsp. fennel seeds, roasted and ground
1 qt. (1 l) Shrimp Stock (page 202) *or*
   Fish Stock (page 201)
½ tsp. saffron threads
½ tsp. sea salt
½ tsp. freshly ground black pepper
4 rouget *or* red mullet fillets
8 green shrimp, shelled and butterflied open
**Preserved lemon gremolata**
2 tsp. finely chopped zest of PRESERVED LEMON
   (page 124)
1 clove garlic, finely chopped
2 tsp. chopped flat-leaf parsley

**1** Preheat oven to hot at 450°F (220°C). Cut tomatoes in half lengthwise, place in a single layer on a sheet pan, and drizzle over 3½ tbsp. (50 ml) of the oil. Roast for about 30 minutes, or until soft and caramelized. **2** Heat remaining oil in a pot over gentle heat and cook onion, garlic, fennel, chili, leek, carrot, and fennel seeds until softened and slightly colored. **3** Add stock, roasted tomatoes, and their juices and bring to the boil. Simmer gently for 20 minutes. Pass through a fine mesh sieve, pressing firmly to extract all juices. Discard solids. **4** Reheat broth to boiling point, add saffron, and season with sea salt and pepper. **5** Make preserved lemon gremolata by mixing all ingredients together in a bowl. **6** Place fish fillets and shrimp on a lightly oiled sheet pan. Season lightly with salt and pepper and grill for 2 to 3 minutes, or until just cooked. **7** Ladle broth into serving bowls and add a fish fillet and 2 shrimp per bowl. Sprinkle with gremolata and serve immediately.

*Serves 4*

## Grilled swordfish with eggplant, tomato, preserved lemon, and olives

one 10 oz. (300 g) eggplant

1¼ cups (300 ml) extra-virgin olive oil

2 tbsp. (30 ml) aged (8- *or* 12-year-old) balsamic vinegar

1 tsp. sea salt

1 tsp. freshly ground black pepper

4 oven-dried tomatoes, cut into thin strips

8 kalamata olives, pitted and sliced

2 tbsp. chervil leaves

2 tbsp. finely sliced zest of PRESERVED LEMON (page 124)

Four ¼ lb. (125 g) swordfish fillets (see Note)

**1** Peel eggplant and cut into thin strips lengthwise. Heat half the oil in a frying pan and fry eggplant for about 15 minutes, or until slightly colored and soft. Remove from heat and set aside. **2** Whisk vinegar in a bowl with salt, pepper, and ⅓ cup (80 ml) of the remaining oil until emulsified. **3** In another bowl, combine fried eggplant, tomato strips, olives, chervil, and PRESERVED LEMON zest. **4** Heat remaining oil in a grilling pan over moderate heat and cook swordfish fillets for 2 to 4 minutes, depending on thickness, until cooked halfway through. Flip fillets over and cook other side. Remove carefully from pan. **5** Arrange vegetable salad on four plates and spoon vinaigrette over. Sit fish on top and serve.

*Serves 4*

Note: Tuna, kingfish, marlin, turbot, monkfish, or mackerel can be substituted for the swordfish.

## Chicken couscous salad with lemon

1 cup (200 g) couscous (see Note)

1⅔ cups (400 ml) White Chicken Stock (page 202)
   *or* water

2 tbsp. unsalted butter

4 oz. (125 g) green beans, sliced diagonally

2 cooked chicken breasts, shredded

2 tbsp. diced zest of PRESERVED LEMON
   (page 124)

12 cherry tomatoes, halved

8 green olives, pitted and sliced

¼ cup shredded flat-leaf parsley

¼ cup mint leaves

1 small red onion, finely chopped

**Vinaigrette**

3½ tbsp. (50 ml) lemon juice

2 tsp. pomegranate molasses *or* honey

2 cloves garlic, finely chopped

¾ cup (175 ml) extra-virgin olive oil

1 tsp. sea salt

1 tsp. freshly ground black pepper

**1** Place couscous in a bowl. Bring stock to the boil and pour over couscous. Stir in butter and leave to stand, stirring occasionally, for 15 minutes, or until liquid has been absorbed. Cool. **2** Blanch beans and refresh in cold water. **3** Make vinaigrette by whisking all ingredients together. **4** In a large bowl, combine couscous, beans, chicken, PRESERVED LEMON zest, tomato, olives, herbs, and onion. Stir in vinaigrette and serve.

*Serves 4*

Note: Cracked wheat may be substituted for the couscous. Soak it in water for 1 hour and then blanch in boiling water for 30 seconds. Drain and allow to cool before using.

4 lamb shanks
¼ cup (60 ml) olive oil
3 tsp. freshly ground black pepper
2 medium onions, finely chopped
6 cloves garlic, finely chopped
1 tbsp. finely chopped ginger
1 Thai chili, finely chopped
1 tsp. ground cumin
1 tsp. ras el hanout spice mix
½ tsp. chili powder *or* paprika
6 cups (1.5 l) Beef/Veal Stock (page 203)
8 small potatoes, thickly sliced
zest of ½ PRESERVED LEMON (page 124), chopped
3 tbsp. (40 ml) lemon juice
¼ cup chervil leaves
mashed potato, steamed rice *or* couscous, to serve

## Lamb shanks with preserved lemon

**1** Preheat oven to low at 300°F (150°C). **2** Brush shanks with some of the oil and sprinkle with 1 tsp. of the pepper. Brown in a large, heavy-bottomed cast-iron casserole over moderately high heat for about 10 minutes each side. Remove meat from pot. **3** Add remaining oil and cook onion, garlic, ginger, and chili until fragrant. Stir in ground spices and remaining pepper and cook for a few minutes. **4** Pour in stock and bring to the boil. Reduce to a simmer, return shanks to pot with potato, and cover with a lid. Place pot in oven and cook slowly, turning meat in the stock during cooking, for about 1½ hours. **5** Stir in PRESERVED LEMON zest and lemon juice. Cook for another 15 minutes, or until meat is very tender, almost falling off the bone. Taste and, if necessary, adjust seasoning. Add chervil as you are about to serve. Serve with mashed potato, steamed rice, or couscous.

*Serves 4*

# Green Masala Paste

The true term for any Indian spice-mix preparation, whether it be wet or dry, is "masala." This is more often referred to in English-speaking countries merely as "curry" – as if it were a generic term for a dish with a one-dimensional flavor. This particular masala paste is versatile, pungent and slightly sour and has its origins in southern India, although the use of vinegar is particular to Goa. It is used in the making of rich sauces and curries and is best suited to fish, chicken or vegetables. It can give indefinable nuances to slow-cooked preparations or simply be stirred into food towards the end of cooking to give a delicious and herbaceous burst of flavor.

## Green masala paste

1⅔ cups (400 ml) malt vinegar

1 tbsp. fenugreek seeds

2 tsp. cumin seeds

3 cups chopped mint leaves

4 cups chopped cilantro leaves

25 cloves garlic, finely chopped

3 tbsp. finely chopped ginger

1 tbsp. finely chopped fresh turmeric (see Note)

2 tbsp. ground turmeric

1 tsp. freshly ground cloves

2 tsp. freshly ground green cardamom seeds

1¼ cups (300 ml) vegetable oil

3½ tbsp. (50 ml) sesame oil

3½ tbsp. (50 ml) fish sauce

**1** Bring malt vinegar and fenugreek seeds to the boil in a stainless steel or enameled saucepan. Remove from heat and set aside for 6 hours, or overnight. **2** Dry-roast cumin seeds over gentle heat until fragrant. Cool, then grind to a fine powder. **3** Process all ingredients, in small batches if necessary, to a smooth, fine paste in an electric blender or food processor. **4** Cook paste in a wide, heavy-bottomed pan over gentle heat for 1 hour, stirring regularly and adding more oil if necessary to prevent sticking. **5** Spoon into sterilized jars, cover with a film of oil, and seal when cool. Keeps, refrigerated, for 1 month.

*Makes about 2½ cups (600 ml)*

Note: If fresh turmeric is unavailable, increase ground turmeric measure by 1 tsp.

13 oz. (400 g) potatoes, peeled and thickly sliced

2 tbsp. ghee

3 cloves garlic, finely chopped

1 tsp. finely chopped ginger

2 small Thai *or* serrano chilies, seeded and
  finely chopped

1 tsp. ground turmeric

24 fresh curry leaves

4 tsp. GREEN MASALA PASTE (page 142)

2 tomatoes, cut into rounds

1 tbsp. brown sugar

2 tsp. sea salt

2 tbsp. fresh peas, blanched

2 tsp. Garam Masala (page 200)

1 tbsp. Fried Shallot Slices (page 201)

## Masala potatoes

**1** Cook potatoes in boiling salted water until just cooked. Drain. **2** Melt ghee in a saucepan and fry garlic, ginger, and chili. Add turmeric, curry leaves, and GREEN MASALA PASTE and fry for about 2 minutes, or until fragrant. **3** Add potato, tomato, sugar, and salt. Simmer on low heat, stirring occasionally, for 10 minutes, or until tomato begins to soften. Add peas and heat through. **4** Remove from heat, sprinkle with garam masala and fried shallot slices, and serve.

*Serves 4*

2 large eggs
1 tsp. fish sauce
2 tsp. ghee
1 tsp. finely diced onion
1 tsp. GREEN MASALA PASTE (page 142)
1 tbsp. bean sprouts
1 tbsp. snow pea sprouts (see Note)
2 tsp. cilantro leaves
1 tsp. Fried Shallot Slices (page 201)

## Individual masala omelettes

1 Whisk eggs and fish sauce in a bowl. 2 Melt ghee in an omelette pan and cook onion until starting to color. Add GREEN MASALA PASTE and fry over moderate heat until fragrant. 3 Add egg mixture to pan, stirring with a spoon or chopstick to combine. When omelette begins to set, add bean sprouts, snow pea sprouts, and cilantro leaves. The omelette is ready when still soft in the center. 4 Fold omelette in half and transfer to a warm plate. Sprinkle fried shallot slices over to serve.

*Serves 1*

Note: If making this dish for more than 1 person, cook an omelette at a time for best results. If snow pea sprouts are unavailable, increase bean sprout measure by 1 tbsp.

## Sour vegetable curry

3 tbsp. (40 ml) vegetable oil
2 small onions, sliced
3 cloves garlic, sliced
2 tsp. finely chopped ginger
2 small green jalapeño chilies, sliced
4 tsp. GREEN MASALA PASTE (page 142)
2 tbsp. chickpea flour (besan)
⅓ cup (100 ml) coconut milk
1⅔ cups (400 ml) Spiced Vegetable Stock (page 204)
⅓ cup (100 ml) Tamarind Liquid (page 200)
1 tbsp. (30 g) brown sugar (*or* palm sugar, shaved)
4 tsp. (20 ml) fish sauce
1 small green mango
4 oz. (100 g) sweet potato, cut into 1 in. (2.5 cm) dice
4 oz. (100 g) small potatoes, halved
1 small carrot, cut into ¾ in. (2 cm) lengths
4 okra
1 fennel bulb, cut into ¾ in. (2 cm) thick slices
2 oz. (50 g) small round eggplants
2 tbsp. mint leaves
2 tbsp. cilantro leaves
steamed rice, to serve

**1** Heat oil in a wide frying pan and fry onion, garlic, ginger, and chili until softened and beginning to color. Stir in GREEN MASALA PASTE and fry for another 2 minutes, or until fragrant. **2** Add flour and cook, stirring constantly, over low heat until paste has thickened. Add coconut milk, stock, tamarind liquid, sugar, and fish sauce and simmer for 10 minutes. **3** Peel mango and discard skin and seed. Cut into 1 in. (2.5 cm) dice. Add to curry with sweet potato and potato and cook for 10 minutes. **4** Add remaining vegetables and simmer for a further 15 to 20 minutes, or until vegetables are cooked. Taste and, if necessary, adjust seasoning. **5** Add mint and cilantro leaves and serve with steamed rice.

*Serves 4*

Note: Water can be used instead of the Spiced Vegetable Stock.

¾ lb. (400 g) long pasta (spaghetti, linguine *or* tagliatelle)

6 tbsp. (75 g) unsalted butter

2 small green jalapeño chilies, finely sliced

2 cloves garlic, finely chopped

2 tsp. GREEN MASALA PASTE (page 142)

1 tbsp. brown sugar

2 tsp. strained lime juice

1 green bell pepper, seeded and finely sliced

2 oz. (50 g) arugula leaves

2 tbsp. chopped cilantro leaves

2 tbsp. chopped Vietnamese mint (laksa) leaves

1 tbsp. snipped chives *or* Chinese chives

1 tbsp. chopped Thai basil leaves

1 tsp. sea salt

1 tsp. freshly ground black pepper

Pasta tossed with herb masala

**1** Cook pasta in boiling water until al dente. Drain. **2** Meanwhile, heat butter in a saucepan and fry chili and garlic for 1 minute. Add GREEN MASALA PASTE and sugar. Cook for 5 minutes over moderate heat. **3** Add cooked pasta, lime juice, bell pepper, arugula, herbs, salt, and pepper. Toss thoroughly to coat pasta with the spice-and-herb mixture. Serve immediately.

*Serves 4*

## Mussels in green masala sauce

2 lb. (1 kg) black mussels, shells scrubbed

2 tbsp. Saffron Butter (page 200)

1 tbsp. finely shredded mint leaves

2 tbsp. diced tomato *or* tomato cut into thin strips

blanched spinach, napa cabbage, *or* roasted
   tomatoes, to serve

**Green masala sauce**

2 tsp. ghee

1 tbsp. diced onion

½ tsp. ground turmeric

4 tsp. GREEN MASALA PASTE (page 142)

4 tsp. SPICED TOMATO CHILI PICKLE (page 108)

8 tsp. tomato purée

⅔ cup (150 ml) Fish Stock (page 201)

2 tsp. brown sugar (*or* palm sugar, shaved)

4 tsp. (20 ml) fish sauce

**1** To make the sauce, melt ghee in a wide, heavy-bottomed saucepan over moderate heat and fry onion until softened. Add turmeric and fry until fragrant, then stir in GREEN MASALA PASTE and SPICED TOMATO CHILI PICKLE. Cook for a few minutes until mixture starts to bubble, then stir in tomato purée and cook for another minute. Add stock and cook gently for 25 minutes, or until slightly thickened. Stir in sugar and fish sauce and cook for 5 minutes, stirring until sugar has dissolved. **2** Toss mussels into a separate wide, heavy-bottomed saucepan over high heat. Cover and steam until shells open. This will take only about 1 minute. Remove open mussels (discard any that haven't opened or are broken) and plunge into ice water to stop the cooking process. Drain. When cool, remove mussels from shells. Discard shells. **3** To serve, bring sauce to the boil and add mussels, saffron butter, mint, and tomato. Stir over moderate heat to work in butter. Taste and, if necessary, adjust seasoning. As soon as butter has been incorporated, remove pan from heat and serve with blanched spinach, napa cabbage, or roasted tomatoes.

*Serves 4*

1 lb. (500 g) green tomatoes

⅓ cup (80 ml) vegetable oil

1 medium onion, finely sliced

4 tsp. GREEN MASALA PASTE (page 142)

2 tsp. sea salt

1 tsp. ground turmeric

1 tsp. chili powder *or* paprika

⅓ cup (100 ml) water

3 tbsp. sugar

## Fried green tomatoes

**1** Slice tomatoes lengthwise into eighths. **2** Heat oil in a large frying pan and add onion and GREEN MASALA PASTE. Cook gently for a few minutes. **3** Add tomato and stir to coat thoroughly with spice paste. Cook over moderate heat for 5 minutes until tomato begins to soften, tossing pan occasionally to prevent sticking. **4** Add salt, turmeric, and chili and toss to combine. Add water and sugar and cook for a further 10 minutes or until water has evaporated. **5** Taste and, if necessary, adjust seasoning. Serve warm.

*Serves 4*

⅞ cup (200 g) thick plain yogurt
1 tsp. ground turmeric
2 tsp. coriander seeds, roasted and ground
4 tsp. GREEN MASALA PASTE (page 142)
1 tbsp. shredded mint leaves
2 tbsp. chickpea flour (besan)
4 chicken thighs, cut in half at the joint
2 tbsp. ghee
2 medium onions, finely sliced
3 tsp. fish sauce
2 tbsp. flaked almonds, lightly toasted
extra shredded mint leaves

## Mint and yogurt chicken

**1** In a bowl, mix yogurt with turmeric, ground coriander, GREEN MASALA PASTE, mint, and flour. Add chicken and marinate, covered, at room temperature for 1 hour. **2** In a wide-bottomed pan, melt ghee and fry onion over moderate heat for about 5 minutes, or until it begins to color. **3** Remove chicken from marinade and fry in pan with onion until chicken begins to color. Add marinade, reduce heat to low, and cook for about 25 minutes, or until chicken is tender. **4** Add fish sauce and cook for another 5 minutes. Taste and, if necessary, adjust seasoning. When chicken is cooked, transfer to a serving plate and sprinkle with almonds and extra mint.

*Serves 4*

## Cilantro Peanut Pesto

This is an Asian version of the more familiar Italian basil pesto, fired up with a touch of chili and some aromatic herbs. Its flavor is redolent of the Orient, with a fresh, heady zing on the palate. Spoon it over hot noodles or pasta, serve it as a condiment with wontons or dumplings or stir it into soups. Like its Italian cousin, this pesto has maximum flavor impact when fresh, so it is best made when there is an abundance of fresh herbs available. Be sure that the peanuts you use are as fresh as possible – taste them in their raw state to double-check – because rancid nuts are not pleasant on the palate. Do not substitute Italian basil pesto in the following recipes; they are specifically designed to partner cilantro peanut pesto.

## Cilantro peanut pesto

¾ cup (200 ml) peanut oil
¼ cup (40 g) raw peanuts, blanched
2 Thai chilies, finely chopped
1 tbsp. finely chopped ginger
8 cloves garlic, finely chopped
2 firmly packed cups Thai basil leaves
½ firmly packed cup Vietnamese mint (laksa) leaves
2 firmly packed cups cilantro leaves
1 tsp. brown sugar (*or* palm sugar, shaved)
2 tsp. fish sauce
4 tsp. (20 ml) strained lime juice

**1** Heat oil in a frying pan and fry peanuts over moderate heat until golden. Strain peanuts, reserving oil, and allow to cool. **2** Blend cooled peanuts in a food processor with chili, ginger, and garlic. Add herbs and half the reserved oil, and blend to a smooth paste. **3** Blend in brown sugar, fish sauce, and lime juice and process until herbs are finely chopped. **4** With motor running, gradually pour in enough of the remaining oil to make a smooth paste. Spoon into a sterilized jar, cover with a film of oil, and seal. Keeps, refrigerated, for up to 2 weeks, but is best used soon after it is made.

*Makes about 1²/₃ cups (400 ml)*

one 7 oz. (200 g) eggplant
1 red bell pepper
1 yellow bell pepper
2 small (pencil) leeks, trimmed
2 small zucchini, sliced lengthwise
2 small waxy potatoes, peeled and sliced
1 large red onion, sliced into thick rings
8 asparagus spears, trimmed and peeled
olive oil
4 tsp. sea salt
2 tsp. freshly ground black pepper
4 tsp. coriander seeds, roasted and ground
½ cup cilantro leaves
4 tbsp. CILANTRO PEANUT PESTO (page 154)

## Grilled vegetables with cilantro

**1** Cut eggplant lengthwise into ½ in. (1 cm) slices. Lightly salt and set aside on a sheet pan for 30 minutes.
**2** Roast bell peppers over direct flame to blacken skins. Peel, discard seeds, and slice flesh into thick strips.
**3** Heat a cast-iron grill pan or barbecue. Brush each piece of vegetable with olive oil. Lay vegetables on a large sheet pan and sprinkle generously with salt, pepper, and ground coriander. **4** Grill vegetables, turning them halfway through cooking time, for 10 to 15 minutes or until softened and cooked. **5** Pile grilled vegetables onto a large, warm plate and sprinkle with cilantro leaves. Pass CILANTRO PEANUT PESTO as a condiment for dipping.

*Serves 4*

½ lb. (200 g) fresh Chinese egg noodles *or*
  spaghettini pasta (see Note)
olive oil
24 large Pacific oysters, unshucked (see Note)
2 oz. (50 g) tatsoi leaves *or* small napa cabbage leaves
2 tsp. pickled ginger, finely sliced
½ cup cilantro leaves
4 scallions, cut into ½ in. (1 cm) lengths
1 large green chili, finely sliced
4 oz. (100 g) snow pea sprouts (see Note)
4 tsp. CILANTRO PEANUT PESTO (page 154)
**Oyster dressing**
⅖ cup (100 ml) Fish Stock (page 201)
4 tsp. (20 ml) Tamarind Liquid (page 200)
3 tbsp. (40 ml) reserved oyster juices, strained
1 tsp. fish sauce
1 tsp. light soy sauce
2 tsp. mirin
2 tsp. strained lime juice

# Pacific oysters stir-fried with cilantro noodles

**1** Blanch noodles briefly in boiling water, then drain and dress with a little olive oil to prevent sticking. **2** Shuck oysters and reserve juices for dressing. Discard shells. **3** To make oyster dressing, mix all ingredients in a bowl. Taste for balance between acid and salt and adjust if necessary. Set aside. **4** Divide all ingredients into four portions. For each serving, put a portion of noodles, tatsoi leaves, and dressing into a bowl and remaining ingredients into another bowl – you should have two bowls for each person (eight in total). Each portion must be cooked separately to ensure perfect cooking. **5** Stand wok (or woks, if you have more than one) over high heat and tip in first portion of noodles, dressing, and tatsoi. Toss until warmed through, being careful that noodles don't stick. Add second bowl of ingredients, stirring with tongs to combine quickly, and toss over heat until warmed through, about 1 minute. Pile onto a plate and serve immediately. **6** Repeat process until all portions are cooked. The number of repeats depends on the number of woks you have. Even if you have only one, the cooking is so quick that the cooked portions can wait without loss of heat or quality while the remaining portions are cooked.

*Serves 4*

Note: If dried noodles are substituted, blanch before using. East Coast oysters may be substituted for Pacific oysters. An equal amount of bean sprouts may be substituted for snow pea sprouts.

## Spiced coconut broth with shellfish and cilantro

2 blue crabs, cleaned and split in half
4 large green king shrimp, shelled and deveined
12 black mussels, steamed open
two ⅜ lb. (200 g) lobster tails, split in half
8 fresh sea scallops
8 napa cabbage hearts, blanched
½ cup cilantro leaves
1 tsp. finely sliced rounds of Thai chili
2 kaffir lime leaves, shredded
4 tsp. CILANTRO PEANUT PESTO (page 154)
4 tsp. Fried Shallot Slices (page 201)

**Spiced coconut broth**
3¼ cups (800 ml) coconut milk
1 tbsp. finely chopped fresh galangal (see Note)
2 tsp. finely chopped ginger
3 Thai chilies, finely chopped
2 cilantro roots, finely chopped
4 shallots, sliced lengthwise
4 kaffir lime leaves, shredded
2 stalks lemongrass, finely chopped
zest of 1 kaffir lime
1⅔ cups (400 ml) Shrimp Stock (page 202)
3½ tbsp. (50 ml) fish sauce
3 tbsp. (40 ml) strained lime juice

**1** To make spiced coconut broth, bring coconut milk to the boil in a saucepan, uncovered, and boil for a few minutes. Add aromatics and simmer for a few minutes. Add stock and fish sauce and simmer on low heat for 15 minutes. Pass broth through a fine mesh sieve and add lime juice. Taste and, if necessary, adjust seasoning. **2** Butterfly shrimp open by cutting down their backs and flattening them. Remove mussels from shells and discard shells. **3** Reheat broth in a wide-bottomed pan and when it starts to boil, add crab. Reduce heat to very low and simmer for 3 minutes. Add shrimp and lobster tails and cook, stirring occasionally, for 3 minutes. Add scallops and mussels and cook for 2 minutes. Remove shellfish from pan with a slotted spoon and place on a warm plate. **4** Add blanched napa cabbage hearts to broth and reheat for 1 minute to warm through. **5** Spoon 2 napa cabbage hearts into center of four serving bowls and divide shellfish between bowls. **6** Stir cilantro, chili, and lime leaves into broth and ladle over shellfish. **7** Add a tsp. of CILANTRO PEANUT PESTO to each bowl and, using a chopstick, swirl into broth. Sprinkle with fried shallot slices and serve.

*Serves 4*

Note: Fish Stock (page 201) can be used instead of Shrimp Stock. Use an additional tablespoon of fresh ginger if galangal is unavailable.

vegetable oil, for deep-frying
8 small fish fillets
8 snow peas, trimmed
4 round slices eggplant
½ green bell pepper, cut into quarters
8 asparagus tips
1 cup Tempura Batter (page 201)
16 tsp. CILANTRO PEANUT PESTO (page 154)
⅓ cup (80 ml) extra-virgin olive oil

Fish and vegetable tempura with
cilantro peanut pesto

**1** Heat vegetable oil in a deep-fryer or large pot to 350°F (180°C). **2** Dip fish pieces and vegetables in tempura batter and fry quickly, in small batches, in hot oil for 2 to 3 minutes or until crispy. Remove with a slotted spoon and set aside to drain on paper towels. Repeat until all fish and vegetables have been cooked. **3** Mix CILANTRO PEANUT PESTO with olive oil and place in dipping bowls. Arrange fish and vegetables on plates and serve immediately.

*Serves 4*

## Roasted chicken and coriander fennel salad

2 tsp. finely chopped cilantro roots
2 tsp. finely chopped garlic
⅓ cup (80 ml) olive oil
1 tsp. freshly ground black pepper
1 tsp. sea salt
1 tsp. fish sauce
8 scallions, finely sliced
One 4½ lb. (2 kg) chicken
2 fennel bulbs, finely shaved
½ cup cilantro leaves
7 oz. (200 g) snow pea sprouts (see Note)
4 tsp. CILANTRO PEANUT PESTO (page 154)

**1** Preheat oven to hot at 450°F (220°C). Mix cilantro root with garlic, oil, pepper, sea salt, fish sauce, and half the scallions. Push some of this paste between skin and meat of chicken and rub the remainder into cavity and over all surfaces. **2** Truss chicken and place in an oiled roasting pan. Roast for 1 hour, or until chicken is golden and juices run clear when thigh is pierced with a skewer. Remove chicken from pan and set aside in a warm place. **3** Add remaining green onion, fennel, cilantro leaves, snow pea sprouts, and CILANTRO PEANUT PESTO to the juices in the pan. Toss to combine until leaves have wilted. **4** Place warm salad on plates. Carve chicken and add to the salad. Serve immediately.

*Serves 4*

Note: Substitute bean sprouts if snow pea sprouts are unavailable.

## Chicken and cilantro broth

4¾ cups (1.2 l) White Chicken Stock (page 202)
2 chicken breasts
⅓ cup (80 ml) light soy sauce
½ tsp. sea salt
½ tsp. freshly ground white pepper
4 eggs, lightly beaten
7 oz. (200 g) bean sprouts
1 tbsp. finely sliced ginger
1 cup watercress leaves
½ cup cilantro leaves
16 tsp. CILANTRO PEANUT PESTO (page 154)

**1** Bring stock to boiling point in a saucepan. Add chicken, cover with a lid, and turn off heat. Leave chicken in hot stock for 20 minutes, then remove and shred meat. **2** Return stock to the boil and flavor with soy sauce, salt, and pepper. **3** Stir egg into boiling stock, swirling with a chopstick to form threads. Remove saucepan from heat. **4** Put shredded chicken, bean sprouts, ginger, watercress, and cilantro leaves into bowls, and ladle broth over. Swirl 4 tsp. CILANTRO PEANUT PESTO into each bowl and serve.

*Serves 4*

Note: To make this soup heartier, add cooked noodles of your choice – somen, thin egg noodles, rice noodles, or angel hair pasta.

4 tsp. (20 ml) peanut oil

2 cloves garlic, minced

1 large red Anaheim *or* Dutch chili, finely sliced

1⅔ cups (400 ml) Fish Stock (page 201) *or* water

½ cup Chinese Shaoxing rice wine

3 tbsp. (40 ml) fish sauce

4½ lb. (2 kg) clams, scrubbed and soaked in cold water
(see Note)

4 tsp. CILANTRO PEANUT PESTO (page 154)

1 cup cilantro leaves

1 cup snow pea sprouts, trimmed (see Note)

3 scallions, finely sliced

4 oz. (100 g) somen noodles, cooked and drained

1 tsp. chili oil

## Clams tossed with cilantro pesto and chili oil

**1** Heat peanut oil in a large, heavy-bottomed pot over medium heat. Fry garlic and chili for a few seconds until fragrant. Add stock, rice wine, and fish sauce. Cover and bring to the boil. Add clams, cover, and bring back to the boil. **2** Reduce heat to a simmer and cook for 5 to 6 minutes or until clams open. Taste and, if necessary, adjust seasoning. Remove from heat and stir in CILANTRO PEANUT PESTO, cilantro leaves, snow pea sprouts, and scallions. **3** Divide noodles equally between four serving bowls and drizzle with a little chili oil. Ladle clams and their broth over noodles and serve immediately.

*Serves 4*

Note: Mussels can be substituted for the clams. They need to be washed and de-bearded before cooking. Substitute bean sprouts if snow pea sprouts are unavailable.

# Massaman Curry Paste

Massaman curry paste is specific to central and southern Thailand and translates as "Muslim curry." It is named after the Malay traders who influenced the foods of the region over the past century. In their turn, they were directly influenced by migrating Indians, so the food has a mixed ancestry. Curries made with this paste are complex, rich and spicy and the inclusion of the Indian spices cardamom and cinnamon provides a wonderful depth of flavor. The paste is usually cooked into coconut cream with thinner coconut milk added at a later stage, along with roasted peanuts. For best results, use with chicken and beef or other rich, red meats. The paste also makes a good base for a spicy, stock-based sauce or a stir-fry, and can transform a marinade.

## Massaman curry paste

4 tsp. cumin seeds

8 tsp. coriander seeds

seeds from 5 green cardamom pods

6 cloves

2 sticks cinnamon

8 dried Thai chilies

2 tsp. Thai shrimp paste (kapi)

6 Thai chilies, chopped

20 cloves garlic, chopped

2 small onions, chopped

4 tsp. fresh green peppercorns

5 cilantro roots, chopped

3½ tbsp. (50 ml) vegetable oil

zest of 2 kaffir limes, finely chopped

2 stalks lemongrass, chopped

⅓ cup (75 g) brown sugar (*or* palm sugar, shaved)

⅓ cup (80 ml) fish sauce

¼ cup (60 ml) Tamarind Liquid (page 200)

**1** Dry-roast cumin, coriander, and cardamom seeds with cloves, cinnamon sticks, and dried chilies over gentle heat until fragrant. Cool, then grind to a fine powder. **2** Dry-roast shrimp paste over gentle heat until fragrant. **3** Blend fresh chili, garlic, onion, peppercorns, cilantro root, and vegetable oil to a fine paste in a food processor. Cook paste over gentle heat in a frying pan until slightly colored and softened. **4** Return hot paste to food processor and blend with lime zest, lemongrass, and dry-roasted shrimp paste. **5** Mix paste, ground spices, and remaining ingredients thoroughly. Spoon into a sterilized jar, cover with a film of oil, and seal when cool. Keeps, refrigerated, for 2 weeks.

*Makes about 1 cup (250 ml)*

1 cup (200 ml) canned coconut cream

1 tbsp. brown sugar (*or* palm sugar, shaved)

4 tsp. (20 ml) fish sauce

2 tsp. MASSAMAN CURRY PASTE (page 166)

2 tsp. SAMBAL BAJAK (page 42)

2 tsp. strained lime juice

24 fresh sea scallops, cleaned

1 large red Anaheim *or* Dutch chili, seeded and
   finely sliced

¼ cup freshly shaved *or* grated coconut

2 scallions, sliced

4 kaffir lime leaves, shredded

4 tbsp. shredded segments of pomelo *or*
   red grapefruit

1 small cucumber, seeded and finely sliced

2 tbsp. cilantro leaves

2 tbsp. shredded Thai basil leaves

¼ cup watercress leaves

2 tbsp. Fried Shallot Slices (page 201)

## Coconut chili scallops with pomelo salad

**1** Bring coconut cream, brown sugar, and fish sauce to the boil in a saucepan, uncovered, then reduce to a simmer and stir in MASSAMAN CURRY PASTE, SAMBAL BAJAK, and lime juice. Cook for 5 minutes. Taste and, if necessary, adjust seasoning. **2** Reduce heat to very low and poach scallops in coconut sauce for 2 to 3 minutes. Remove scallops from sauce and remove sauce from heat. **3** Mix all remaining ingredients, except fried shallot slices, in a bowl. Add scallops and coconut sauce and toss to combine. **4** Pile warm scallop salad onto serving plates, positioning scallops on top. Sprinkle with fried shallots and serve immediately.

*Serves 4*

two 2 lb. (1 kg) live rock lobsters (see Note)

8 tsp. MASSAMAN CURRY PASTE (page 166)

1 tsp. CHILI JAM (page 6)

¾ cup (200 ml) coconut milk

3½ tbsp. (50 ml) tomato purée

2 tbsp. (30 ml) fish sauce

8 fresh banana leaves (see Note)

¼ cup Fried Shallot Slices (page 201)

2 large red Anaheim *or* Dutch chilies, split lengthwise,
    seeded and deep-fried

## Spicy masala lobster

**1** Stun lobsters in freezer for 30 minutes, then plunge briefly into a stockpot of rapidly boiling water (this is to kill rather than cook them). **2** Remove lobster tail meat and discard heads, shells and claws (use them to make stock for another recipe). Cut each lobster tail in half lengthwise. **3** Preheat oven to moderately hot at 400°F (200°C). **4** Bring MASSAMAN CURRY PASTE, CHILI JAM, coconut milk, tomato purée, and fish sauce to a simmer in a saucepan, stirring to combine. Allow to cool. **5** Coat lobster liberally with cooled sauce and pile into tail halves. Wrap each piece of tail in a banana leaf, folding over to secure. **6** Bake the four parcels seam-side down for 8 to 10 minutes, or until meat is just cooked. Unwrap and spoon a little sauce over lobster to moisten it. **7** Spread remaining banana leaves on four plates, add a masala lobster tail and its sauce to each plate, and garnish with fried shallots and deep-fried chili. Serve immediately.

*Serves 4*

Note: This recipe also works with crayfish or langoustines. Banana leaves are also available frozen.

1¼ cups (300 ml) coconut milk
⅔ cup (150 ml) Fish Stock (page 201)
4 tsp. (20 ml) fish sauce
8 tsp. MASSAMAN CURRY PASTE (page 166)
2 tsp. CHILI JAM (page 6)
2 tsp. strained lime juice
four 5 oz. (150 g) white fish fillets
½ cup cilantro leaves
steamed rice *or* stir-fried green vegetables, to serve

## Steamed fish with red chili paste

**1** In a saucepan, heat coconut milk, stock, fish sauce, MASSAMAN CURRY PASTE, and CHILI JAM together to boiling point, uncovered. Simmer for 5 minutes. Remove from heat and stir in lime juice. Taste and, if necessary, adjust seasoning. Allow to cool completely. **2** Place fish fillets in a large, shallow bowl in a single layer and pour over half the cooled sauce. Place bowl in a large steamer pan, cover with a lid, and steam over boiling water for 8 to 12 minutes, depending on the size and type of fish used. Test fish with a skewer or knife to check that it is cooked. The flesh should be white and firm without being dry or breaking open. **3** Boil remaining sauce in a saucepan, uncovered, for 5 minutes. **4** Carefully slide fish fillets onto plates, spoon sauce over, and top with cilantro leaves. Serve with steamed rice or stir-fried green vegetables. A spicy rice pilaf or wilted spinach are also good accompaniments.

*Serves 4*

4 chicken thighs, cut in half at the joint
2 tsp. Chinese Five-spice Powder (page 200)
1 tsp. sea salt
3 tbsp. (40 ml) vegetable oil
8 shallots, peeled
1¼ cups (300 ml) canned coconut cream
8 tsp. MASSAMAN CURRY PASTE (page 166)
1¼ cups (300 ml) Brown Chicken Stock (page 202)
4 tsp. (20 ml) fish sauce
3 tbsp. (40 ml) Tamarind Liquid (page 200)
1 tbsp. brown sugar (*or* palm sugar, shaved)
8 small waxy potatoes, peeled and halved
2 tbsp. peanuts, blanched and roughly chopped
½ cup Thai basil leaves
steamed rice and pickled vegetables, to serve

## Chicken and potato curry

**1** Season chicken with five-spice powder and salt. Heat oil in a large saucepan and fry chicken on both sides for about 6 minutes, or until browned. Set aside. **2** In the same pan, fry whole shallots until they begin to color. Add coconut cream and bring to the boil. Simmer for a few minutes until coconut cream appears oily, then stir in MASSAMAN CURRY PASTE and simmer gently for a further 5 minutes. **3** Add stock, fish sauce, tamarind liquid, and brown sugar and bring to the boil. Add potato and simmer for 10 minutes. **4** Add browned chicken, cover, and cook for another 40 minutes on low heat, or until chicken is tender and potato is soft. Stir occasionally to ensure meat is kept coated with sauce. **5** Stir in peanuts and basil and serve with steamed rice and pickled vegetables.

*Serves 4*

4 large quails
8 tsp. MASSAMAN CURRY PASTE (page 166)
vegetable oil, for deep-frying
7 oz. (200 g) small spinach leaves
2 cloves garlic, finely chopped
2 tsp. fish sauce
½ tsp. freshly ground black pepper
2 tbsp. Fried Shallot Slices (page 201)

## Deep-fried spiced quails

**1** Preheat oven to hot at 450°F (220°C). Wash quails and pat dry with paper towels. Rub MASSAMAN CURRY PASTE into cavity of each bird and onto outer surfaces, covering generously. **2** Heat oil in a deep-fryer or large pot to 350°F (180°C). Deep-fry quails for 4 minutes. Transfer to a sheet pan and bake for a further 3 minutes. Remove quails from oven and rest for 2 minutes before serving. **3** Stir-fry spinach in a little oil with garlic, fish sauce, and pepper for about 1 minute, or until wilted. **4** Place some spinach in the center of each serving plate, sit a quail on top, and sprinkle with fried shallot slices to serve.

*Serves 4*

## Rich beef curry

4 tsp. (20 ml) vegetable oil
2 medium onions, finely sliced lengthwise
4 cloves garlic, sliced
2 small Thai *or* serrano chilies, sliced
3¼ cups (800 ml) coconut milk
12 tsp. MASSAMAN CURRY PASTE (page 166)
1 stalk lemongrass, cut into 2 in. (5 cm) lengths
2 kaffir lime leaves
2 tsp. ground turmeric
⅓ cup (80 ml) Tamarind Liquid (page 200)
3 tbsp. (40 ml) light soy sauce
2 lb. (1 kg) chuck *or* blade steak, cut in 2 in. (5 cm) cubes
7 oz. (200 g) pumpkin, cut into 1 in. (2.5 cm) cubes
4 tsp. (20 ml) fish sauce
½ cup cilantro leaves
steamed rice, to serve

**1** Heat oil in a large pot and fry onion, garlic, and chili until beginning to color. **2** Add coconut milk, MASSAMAN CURRY PASTE, lemongrass, lime leaves, turmeric, tamarind liquid, and soy sauce. Bring to the boil and simmer, uncovered, for 5 minutes. **3** Add meat and cook, stirring regularly, on very gentle heat for 1 hour. **4** Add pumpkin and, if too much of the sauce has been absorbed, a little water. Cook for another hour or until pumpkin is soft and the curry is quite dry in appearance, with most of the liquid having been absorbed by the meat. **5** Season with fish sauce. Taste and, if necessary, adjust seasoning. **6** Sprinkle with cilantro leaves and serve with steamed rice.

*Serves 4*

Note: The longer and slower you cook this curry, the better its flavor and texture. Like most curries, it is even better made a day or two in advance and reheated gently to serve.

1 small onion, finely chopped

2 cloves garlic, finely chopped

1 tsp. finely chopped fresh galangal *or* ginger

1 tsp. chili powder *or* paprika

2 tsp. Garam Masala (page 200)

2 tsp. sea salt

1 tsp. freshly ground black pepper

1⅓ lb. (600 g) lean ground beef *or* lamb

2 tbsp. finely chopped flat-leaf parsley

1 tbsp. cilantro leaves, chopped

1 egg

2 tbsp. breadcrumbs

all-purpose flour, for dusting

**Curry sauce**

⅓ cup (100 ml) canned coconut cream

⅓ cup (100 ml) tomato purée

8 tsp. MASSAMAN CURRY PASTE (page 166)

2 tsp. CHILI JAM (page 6)

1¼ cups (300 ml) Beef/Veal Stock (page 203)

2 tsp. light soy sauce

2 tsp. fish sauce

2 tsp. strained lime juice

## Spiced meatballs with curry sauce

**1** To make meatballs, blend onion, garlic, galangal, dry spices, salt, pepper, meat, herbs, egg, and bread-crumbs in a food processor until smooth and combined. Roll into small balls and then roll each ball in a little flour to prevent sticking. **2** To make sauce, heat coconut cream with tomato purée, MASSAMAN CURRY PASTE, and CHILI JAM and bring to the boil. Cook for 10 minutes, uncovered, on moderate heat. Add stock, soy sauce, and fish sauce and simmer for 20 minutes. Add lime juice. Taste and, if necessary, adjust seasoning. Strain sauce through muslin or a fine mesh sieve and discard solids. Pour into a clean pot. **3** Heat a little oil in a large frying pan and fry meatballs in batches for about 10 minutes, or until well browned on all sides. Add meatballs to curry sauce and cook, stirring occasionally, over low heat for 15 minutes. Serve with a rice pilaf or steamed rice.

*Serves 4*

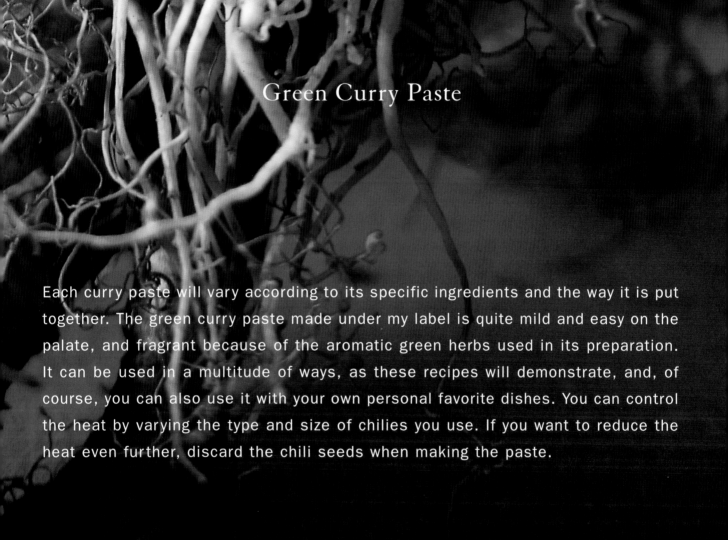

# Green Curry Paste

Each curry paste will vary according to its specific ingredients and the way it is put together. The green curry paste made under my label is quite mild and easy on the palate, and fragrant because of the aromatic green herbs used in its preparation. It can be used in a multitude of ways, as these recipes will demonstrate, and, of course, you can also use it with your own personal favorite dishes. You can control the heat by varying the type and size of chilies you use. If you want to reduce the heat even further, discard the chili seeds when making the paste.

## Green curry paste

1 tsp. Thai shrimp paste (kapi)
1 tsp. coriander seeds
½ tsp. cumin seeds
20 Thai chilies, roughly chopped
5 shallots, chopped
6 cloves garlic, chopped
2 stalks lemongrass, chopped
4 tsp. chopped fresh galangal *or* ginger
8 tsp. chopped fresh cilantro root
½ cup cilantro leaves
¼ cup Thai basil leaves
1 tsp. chopped kaffir lime zest
3 tsp. fresh green peppercorns
¼ tsp. freshly grated nutmeg
2 tsp. fish sauce
4 tsp. water

**1** Dry-roast shrimp paste, coriander seeds, and cumin seeds separately over gentle heat until fragrant. Cool, then combine and grind to a fine powder. **2** Blend all ingredients to a fine paste in a food processor. Spoon into a sterilized jar, cover with a film of oil, and seal when cool. Keeps, refrigerated, for up to 2 weeks. *Makes ¾ cup (200 ml)*

1 lb. (500 g) mixed green vegetables (asparagus, beans,
   snow peas, broccoli, zucchini – whatever is in season)
1 bunch spinach
8 fresh tofu squares
1¼ cups (300 ml) coconut milk
8 tsp. GREEN CURRY PASTE (page 178)
8 kaffir lime leaves
1¼ cups (300 ml) Spiced Vegetable Stock (page 204)
4 tsp. (20 ml) fish sauce
2 tsp. strained lime juice
½ cup Thai basil leaves
½ cup cilantro parsley leaves
boiled *or* steamed rice, to serve

## Green vegetable curry with tofu

**1** Prepare green vegetables by slicing or cutting into uniform thickness to ensure even cooking. Wash spinach in cold water and remove and discard stalks. Cut each tofu square into quarters. **2** Heat coconut milk to boiling point in a saucepan and stir in GREEN CURRY PASTE and lime leaves. Simmer gently, uncovered, for 5 minutes. Add stock, fish sauce, and lime juice and simmer for a further 10 minutes. Taste and, if necessary, adjust seasoning. **3** Add prepared vegetables and cook for 6 to 10 minutes, or until vegetables are soft but not mushy. Add spinach leaves and allow to wilt in the sauce. **4** Carefully stir in tofu pieces with basil and cilantro leaves. Heat through for 2 minutes, then serve with boiled or steamed rice.

*Serves 4*

## Turmeric lemongrass broth with noodles and vegetables

7 oz. (200 g) fresh Egg Noodles (page 204) *or* ramen noodles *or* purchased egg noodles

2 large red Anaheim *or* Dutch chilies, seeded and finely sliced

1 zucchini, cut into julienne

6 scallions, finely sliced

4 oz. (100 g) bean sprouts

1 small carrot, peeled and cut into julienne

4 shiitake mushrooms, finely sliced

4 tsp. finely shredded mint leaves

**Turmeric lemongrass broth**

8 tsp. GREEN CURRY PASTE (page 178)

2 tsp. finely chopped ginger

1 stalk lemongrass, chopped

2 tsp. ground turmeric

2 tsp. vegetable oil

1 qt. (1 l) Spiced Vegetable Stock (page 204)

¾ cup (200 ml) Tamarind Liquid (page 200)

⅓ cup (80 ml) light soy sauce

2 tsp. lemon juice, strained

¼ cup (60 ml) Sugar Syrup (page 201) *or* 2 tbsp. sugar

1 tsp. freshly ground white pepper

**1** To make broth, fry GREEN CURRY PASTE, ginger, lemongrass, and turmeric in vegetable oil for 5 minutes, or until fragrant. Add remaining broth ingredients, except pepper, and bring to the boil. Reduce heat and simmer for 10 minutes. Strain through a fine mesh sieve and discard solids. Reheat broth in a clean pot and stir in pepper. **2** Cook noodles in boiling water, then drain and divide between four bowls. Combine chili and vegetables and add to noodles. Ladle hot broth into bowls to cover noodles and vegetables. Stir with a chopstick. **3** Sprinkle mint on top and serve immediately.

*Serves 4*

## Green curry fish soup

2 cups (500 ml) coconut milk
8 tsp. GREEN CURRY PASTE (page 178)
3 cups (750 ml) Fish Stock (page 201) *or* water
3 tbsp. (40 ml) fish sauce
4 white fish fillets, cut into thick strips
20 small shrimp, shelled and deveined
12 fish balls (available from Asian food stores)
2 tbsp. cilantro leaves
4 kaffir lime leaves, finely shredded
1 tbsp. shredded mint leaves
8 Whole Roasted Shallots (page 201)
8 oz. (250 g) bean sprouts

**1** Heat coconut milk to boiling point. Stir in GREEN CURRY PASTE and cook for 5 minutes on moderate heat, uncovered. Add stock and fish sauce. Bring to the boil, reduce heat, and simmer for 15 minutes. Taste and, if necessary, adjust seasoning. **2** Add fish pieces, shrimp, and fish balls and simmer on very low heat for 3 to 4 minutes, just enough to cook the fish. **3** Remove fish, shrimp, and fish balls from pot with a slotted spoon and divide among four bowls. Distribute remaining ingredients among bowls, pour hot soup over, and serve.

*Serves 4*

sea salt

1 lb. (500 g) pork belly *or* spareribs, cut into 2 in. (5 cm)
  strips

4 tsp. (20 ml) vegetable oil

8 tsp. GREEN CURRY PASTE (page 178)

4 kaffir lime leaves

2 stalks lemongrass, cut into 2 in. (5 cm) lengths

4 slices fresh galangal *or* ginger

1 tsp. minced ginger

2½ cups (625 ml) coconut milk

⅓ cup (100 ml) Tamarind Liquid (page 200)

2 tsp. brown sugar (*or* palm sugar, shaved)

4 tsp. (20 ml) fish sauce

2 small green jalapeño chilies, seeded and sliced

½ cup cilantro leaves

8 Whole Roasted Shallots (page 201)

steamed rice, to serve

## Green curry of pork

**1** Rub salt lightly into pork and refrigerate on a covered pan for 1 hour. **2** Blanch pork in boiling water for 2 minutes, then remove from pot with a slotted spoon and set aside. **3** Heat oil in a wok over high heat and fry GREEN CURRY PASTE, lime leaves, lemongrass, galangal, and ginger, stirring constantly, for 2 minutes or until mixture begins to color. Add pork and coat thoroughly with paste. **4** Stir in coconut milk, tamarind liquid, brown sugar, and fish sauce. Reduce heat to low and simmer, uncovered and stirring occasionally, for 25 to 30 minutes or until pork is tender and liquid has evaporated slightly. **5** Add chili, cilantro leaves, and roasted shallots. Taste and, if necessary, adjust seasoning. Serve with steamed rice.

*Serves 4*

Note: Pork belly (as opposed to a leaner cut like shoulder or neck) is necessary for this dish as a fair degree of fat is needed to give a tender final result.

1 cup (250 ml) canned coconut cream
4 tsp. GREEN CURRY PASTE (page 178)
2 tsp. fish sauce
¾ cup (200 ml) Shrimp Stock (page 202)
16 green tiger shrimp, shelled
1 cup Thai basil leaves, shredded
5 oz. (150 g) small spinach leaves, washed
2 tsp. olive oil

## Tiger shrimp with green coconut curry

**1** Heat coconut cream to simmering point, stir in GREEN CURRY PASTE and fish sauce, and cook over moderate heat for 10 minutes. **2** Add stock and bring to the boil. Simmer for 10 minutes. Taste and, if necessary, adjust seasoning. **3** Add shrimp to sauce and simmer on low heat for 3 to 4 minutes, just long enough so the shrimp change color without overcooking and toughening. **4** Add basil leaves. **5** Wilt spinach in a pan with oil and place on center of plates. Sit shrimp on top and spoon sauce over.

*Serves 4*

3 qt. (3 l) White Chicken Stock (page 202)
1 tsp. sea salt
1 tsp. freshly ground white pepper
one 4 lb. (1.8 kg) free-range chicken
2 scallions
3 slices ginger
1 cup (250 ml) coconut milk
8 tsp. GREEN CURRY PASTE (page 178)
2 tsp. fish sauce
7 oz. (200 g) small spinach leaves, washed
1 bunch Chinese celery (kun choy) *or* plain celery
½ cup cilantro leaves

# White-cooked chicken with green curry sauce

**1** Heat stock to boiling point in a large pot. Rub salt and pepper into skin and cavity of chicken and stuff scallions and ginger into cavity. Tie legs together with string. **2** Place trussed chicken into hot stock, turn off heat, and leave to cook slowly in the stock for 1 hour. Check thigh joint with a skewer – if juices run pale pink, the chicken is ready. If not quite ready, leave in the stock a little longer. Remove chicken from pot and set aside in a warm place. Strain stock through a fine mesh sieve or muslin and set aside. **3** Heat coconut milk to boiling point, stir in GREEN CURRY PASTE and fish sauce, and cook for 5 minutes, uncovered. Add ¾ cup (200 ml) of reserved stock and cook for a further 10 minutes. (Keep remaining stock for another use.) Taste and, if necessary, adjust seasoning. **4** Joint chicken, then cut meat from the bones into thick slices. **5** Bring a saucepan of water to the boil and blanch spinach leaves and celery until wilted, about 30 seconds. Squeeze dry, then divide between four plates. Spoon over the green curry sauce. Sit a few slices of chicken on top of spinach, sprinkle with cilantro leaves, and serve immediately.

*Serves 4*

# Red Curry Paste

Like the green and Massaman curry pastes, this fragrant, sweet and spicy curry paste draws its inspiration and unique flavor combination from Thailand. The flavors have become so familiar in Australia that they are now considered by most people to be a staple in the pantry. For the intriguing depth of flavor of this paste, it is essential that you include Thai shrimp paste (kapi). This single ingredient gives the paste its unique and mysterious pungency. Apart from its obvious uses, try using red curry paste for grilling, or spiking the flavor of meatballs or a baked meatloaf, or as a marinade or to add flavor to a soup. Like its green counterpart, its heat intensity varies according to the number and size of chilies used, so the outcome can be controlled by the maker. Add a few extra chilies if you prefer your paste fiery-hot.

## Red curry paste

6 large dried Anaheim *or* cayenne chilies, chopped

3½ tbsp. (50 ml) warm water

2 tsp. Thai shrimp paste (kapi)

1 tsp. cilantro seeds

½ tsp. white peppercorns, ground

6 shallots, chopped

6 Thai chilies, finely chopped

6 cloves garlic, chopped

2 tsp. finely chopped ginger

1 tbsp. finely chopped fresh galangal (see Note)

1 stalk lemongrass, chopped

1 tsp. finely chopped kaffir lime zest

1 tbsp. chopped cilantro root

4 tsp. CHILI JAM (page 6)

2 tbsp. (30 ml) fish sauce

**1** Soak dried chili in warm water for 15 minutes. **2** Meanwhile, dry-roast shrimp paste and cilantro seeds separately over gentle heat until fragrant. Cool, then grind cilantro seeds to a fine powder. **3** Process all ingredients to a smooth paste in an electric blender or food processor. **4** Spoon into a sterilized jar, cover with a film of oil, and seal. Keeps, refrigerated, for 2 months.

*Makes about ¾ cup (200 ml)*

Note: Add another 1 tbsp. finely chopped ginger if galangal is unavailable.

1 cup chopped pineapple
1 tsp. freshly ground black pepper
vegetable oil
8 tsp. RED CURRY PASTE (page 188)
1 tbsp. brown sugar (*or* palm sugar, shaved)
1⅔ cups (400 ml) coconut milk
½ cup (100 ml) Fish Stock (page 201) *or* water
24 large green tiger shrimp, shelled and deveined
4 tsp. (20 ml) fish sauce
½ cup shredded mint leaves
4 kaffir lime leaves, finely shredded
4 scallions, finely sliced
sticky white rice, to serve

## Sweet shrimp curry

**1** Purée half the chopped pineapple and add pepper. Heat a little oil in a saucepan and fry RED CURRY PASTE, brown sugar, and peppered pineapple for a few minutes, or until fragrant. **2** Add coconut milk and stock and bring to the boil. Simmer on low heat for 10 minutes, uncovered. **3** Add remaining chopped pineapple and simmer for 5 minutes. Add shrimp and fish sauce and cook for 4 to 5 minutes, or until shrimp are just cooked. Taste and, if necessary, adjust seasoning. **4** Stir in mint, lime leaves, and scallion slices. Serve with sticky white rice.

*Serves 4*

## Sautéed chili shrimp

4 tsp. (20 ml) vegetable oil
1 medium onion, sliced thickly lengthwise
1 tsp. CHILI JAM (page 6)
4 tsp. RED CURRY PASTE (page 188)
20 cherry tomatoes
20 large green shrimp, shelled and deveined
4 tsp. (20 ml) strained lime juice
2 tsp. fish sauce
2 tbsp. sugar
4 scallions, finely sliced
coconut rice (nasi lemak), to serve (see Note)

**1** Heat oil in a large wok and fry onion until soft. Add CHILI JAM and RED CURRY PASTE and cook for about 2 minutes. **2** Add tomatoes and shrimp and toss over high heat until shrimp begin to change color. **3** Add lime juice, fish sauce, and sugar and cook for another minute. Taste and, if necessary, adjust seasoning. Remove from heat and pile onto plates. **4** Sprinkle with scallions and serve with coconut rice.

*Serves 4*

Note: To make coconut rice, simply cook jasmine rice in the usual way but substitute coconut milk for water.

## Fried Spanish mackerel with red curry sauce

1 cup (250 ml) canned coconut cream

8 tsp. RED CURRY PASTE (page 188)

2 tsp. fish sauce

1 tbsp. dried shrimp, ground

1 tsp. sugar

4 Chinese long beans, cut into 1 in. (2.5 cm) lengths (see Note)

2 red Anaheim *or* Dutch chilies, finely sliced
vegetable oil, for deep-frying

1⅓ lb. (600 g) Spanish mackerel cutlets *or* fillets

2 tbsp. Thai basil leaves

2 kaffir lime leaves, finely shredded
steamed rice, to serve

**1** Heat coconut cream to simmering point in a saucepan. Add RED CURRY PASTE, fish sauce, dried shrimp, and sugar. Stir. Cook for 10 minutes over moderate heat, uncovered. **2** Add beans and chili and cook for another 3 minutes. Taste and, if necessary, adjust seasoning. **3** Heat oil to 350°F (180°C) in a deep-fryer or large pot and fry fish pieces for 6 to 8 minutes, or until golden and crispy. Drain on paper towels. **4** To serve, place fish on four warmed plates and spoon sauce over. Scatter some basil leaves and lime leaves over top. Serve with steamed rice.

*Serves 4*

Note: Regular green beans may be substituted if Chinese long beans are unavailable.

one 3 lb. (1.5 kg) whole fish, scaled and gutted

4 tsp. (20 ml) strained lime juice

½ tsp. sea salt

½ tsp. freshly ground black pepper

8 tsp. RED CURRY PASTE (page 188)

4 tsp. tomato purée

3 tbsp. (40 ml) vegetable oil

steamed *or* fried rice, to serve

## Grilled spicy fish

**1** With a sharp knife, cut a few diagonal slits about 1 in. (2.5 cm) deep into both sides of fish. (This ensures even cooking time and maximum penetration of spice paste during cooking.) Season inside cavity of fish with lime juice, salt, and pepper. **2** Combine RED CURRY PASTE and tomato purée in a bowl. Fill inside cavity of fish with this and rub some over outer surfaces. Marinate for 2 to 3 hours. **3** Brush fish generously with oil to prevent sticking and place in a hinged wire fish griller (to keep fish together during cooking). Grill or barbecue over moderate heat for 12 to 14 minutes, turning fish after 8 minutes or so. Cooking time will depend on size and type of fish used. Check with a skewer at the thickest part of the flesh. It should be white and firm without being dry or breaking open. **4** Remove fish from heat, lift from the wire griller, and transfer carefully to a serving plate (lined with a fresh banana leaf, if desired). Serve with steamed or fried rice.

*Serves 4*

Note: Banana leaves are also available frozen.

## Roasted duck and eggplant curry

¾ cup (200 ml) canned coconut cream

8 tsp. RED CURRY PASTE (page 188)

4 tsp. (20 ml) fish sauce

¾ cup (200 ml) coconut milk

2 ripe tomatoes, quartered

vegetable oil, for deep-frying

1 large eggplant, about 13 oz. (400 g), diced
    *or* cut into strips

2 large red Anaheim *or* Dutch chilies, split lengthwise
    and seeded

one 4 to 5 lb. (1.8 to 2.2 kg) Chinese roasted duck, cut
    into bite-size chunks (discard bones)

4 kaffir lime leaves, finely shredded

steamed rice, to serve

½ cup Thai basil leaves

**1** Heat coconut cream in a pot and, when boiling, add RED CURRY PASTE and fish sauce. Simmer gently, uncovered, for 10 minutes. **2** Add coconut milk and tomato and simmer for another 10 minutes. **3** Heat oil to 350°F (180°C) in a deep-fryer or large pot and fry eggplant in batches for 4 minutes, or until golden. Drain on paper towels. **4** Deep-fry chili halves for 1 minute, or until slightly colored. Drain on paper towels. **5** Add roasted duck chunks to curry, stir, and cook gently until duck is heated through. Add lime leaves, fried eggplant, and chili. Stir to combine. **6** Remove from heat and serve with steamed rice, garnished with basil leaves.

*Serves 4*

## Combination fried rice

vegetable oil

1 small onion, diced

2 cloves garlic, finely chopped

4 tsp. RED CURRY PASTE (page 188)

2 tsp. sugar

½ lb. (200 g) cooked shrimp, shelled

¼ lb. (100 g) cooked chicken, shredded

¼ lb. (100 g) Chinese red roasted pork slices (cha siew)

3 eggs, beaten

4½ cups (800 g) cooked jasmine (long-grain) rice

3 tbsp. (40 ml) fish sauce

1 red bell pepper, finely chopped

1 oz. (40 g) green beans, sliced into fine rounds

4 scallions, finely sliced

½ cup Thai basil leaves

¼ cup cilantro leaves

2 tbsp. Fried Shallot Slices (page 201)

**1** Heat a little oil in a large wok and fry onion and garlic until starting to color. Add RED CURRY PASTE and sugar and stir to combine. **2** Add shrimp, chicken, and pork and toss over heat to combine. Transfer from wok to a large plate. **3** Heat a little more oil in the wok and add eggs. Cook until they begin to scramble. As they begin to set, stir in rice and fry for about 2 minutes, or until heated through. Add fish sauce, red bell pepper, and beans. **4** Return shrimp mixture to wok and toss to combine thoroughly. Stir in scallions, basil, and cilantro and remove from heat. **5** Arrange fried rice on a serving plate and sprinkle with fried shallot slices.

*Serves 4*

Note: Vary this recipe by using lobster meat instead of shrimp. Another option: Substitute cooked, thinly sliced beef or lamb fillet or ham for the chicken and pork. Fried slices of Chinese (lap cheong) or Thai pork sausage are also a delicious addition.

1⅔ cups (400 ml) coconut milk
⅓ cup (80 ml) Tamarind Liquid (page 200)
8 tsp. RED CURRY PASTE (page 188)
⅞ lb. (400 g) beef topside, cut into 1 in. (2.5 cm) cubes
1 stalk lemongrass, cut into 2 in. (5 cm) lengths
2 kaffir lime leaves
1qt. (1 l) Beef/Veal Stock (page 203)
4 tsp. (20 ml) fish sauce
1 tbsp. sugar
1 cup (200 g) fresh bamboo shoots, sliced lengthwise
2 large red Anaheim *or* Dutch chilies, sliced
¼ cup Thai basil leaves

## Red curry beef soup

1 Bring coconut milk, tamarind liquid, and RED CURRY PASTE to boiling point in a pot. Simmer uncovered, stirring constantly, for 5 minutes. 2 Add beef, lemongrass, and lime leaves. Reduce heat to a low simmer and cook gently for 40 minutes. 3 Add stock, fish sauce, and sugar and return to simmering point. Continue to simmer for another 30 minutes, or until beef is very tender. Taste and, if necessary, adjust seasoning. 4 Add bamboo shoots and chili and cook for 15 minutes. 5 Ladle soup into bowls, top with basil and serve.

*Serves 4*

# Basics

The following preparations are used at various times throughout this book. Most of them are standbys with which good cooks need to be familiar. Making and freezing stock when you can, preparing sauces from summer produce for winter use, and keeping sugar syrup and tamarind liquid at the ready mean that your culinary repertoire can expand as if by magic. If you put the effort in when you have the time, you can reap the benefits when you don't – and enjoy the fruits of your labors.

## CHINESE FIVE-SPICE POWDER

5 star anise
4 tsp. fennel seeds
4 tsp. Sichuan peppercorns
2 tsp. cloves
1 tsp. ground cassia
1 tsp. freshly ground cinnamon

Grind spices to a fine powder, then pass through a fine mesh sieve and discard husks. Store in a sealed jar.
*Makes about 4 tbsp.*

Note: Ready-made Chinese five-spice powder is also available commercially. Cassia can be found at Indian import markets.

## SICHUAN SPICE SALT

2 tbsp. sea salt
2 tsp. Sichuan peppercorns
1 tsp. Chinese five-spice powder (see above)

Dry-roast sea salt and peppercorns over gentle heat until fragrant and lightly colored. Cool. Grind to a fine powder, then pass through a fine mesh sieve and discard husks. Mix with five-spice powder and store in a sealed jar.
*Makes about 3 tbsp.*

Note: Ready-made Sichuan spice salt is also available commercially.

## GARAM MASALA

seeds from 16 green cardamom pods
1 tsp. nigella seeds
1 tsp. cloves
2 tsp. black peppercorns
¼ tsp. freshly grated nutmeg
¼ tsp. ground cassia

Grind whole spices to a fine powder, then stir in remaining spices. Store in a sealed jar.
*Makes about 2 tbsp.*

Note: Ready-made garam masala is also available commercially. Cassia and nigella seeds can be found at Indian import markets.

## SWEET CHILI SAUCE

¾ cup (200 ml) Sugar Syrup (page 201)
⅔ cup (160 ml) strained lime juice
⅓ cup (80 ml) fish sauce
2 tsp. chopped Thai chili
2 tsp. minced garlic

Combine ingredients and refrigerate until ready to use. Keeps, refrigerated, for up to 1 week.
*Makes about 1⅔ cups (400 ml)*

Note: Ready-made sweet chili sauce is also available commercially.

## TAMARIND LIQUID

The most refined way to use tamarind is to make tamarind liquid, getting maximum flavor without the coarse, fibrous texture of the pulp. Simmer 1 part tamarind pulp to 4 parts water for 30 minutes or so, then pass pulp and water through a coarse mesh or conical sieve. Discard fiber and seeds. Tamarind liquid keeps, refrigerated, for up to 1 month.

## SAFFRON BUTTER

Stir into sauces at the last minute to enrich flavor.

3½ tbsp. (50 ml) Tomato Essence (see below)
½ tsp. saffron threads
2 sticks (250 g) unsalted butter, softened

Bring tomato essence to the boil in a small saucepan, add saffron, and infuse for a few minutes only. Whip butter in a food processor and gradually blend in saffron liquid until incorporated. Keeps, refrigerated in a sealed container, for 1 week.
*Makes 16 tbsp. (250 g)*

## TOMATO ESSENCE

An exquisite way of adding the intense flavor of summer's best tomatoes to sauces and the like, and a great way of extending the season, via freezing. Pulp tomatoes and drain in a jelly bag or double layer of muslin suspended over a bowl for 24 hours. To keep essence clear, do not push or force pulp through bag. To make reduced tomato essence, bring essence to the boil and reduce by half. This increases the sweetness slightly and intensifies the flavor. Freeze in ice-cube trays for later use. (Use the remaining pulp as tomato purée.)

*5 lb. (2.5 kg) tomatoes yield about 2 cups (500 ml) essence*

## SUGAR SYRUP

Bring an equal quantity of sugar and water to the boil and cook for about 5 minutes, or until sugar has dissolved. Cool. Sugar syrup keeps indefinitely and can also be made with brown sugar. If preferred, you can substitute 4 tsp. sugar for each 2 tbsp. (30 ml) sugar syrup called for in a recipe.

*1 cup water and 1 cup sugar yield about 1½ cups sugar syrup*

## TEMPURA BATTER

¾ cup all-purpose flour
1 egg, lightly beaten
¾ cup (200 ml) iced soda water
½ tsp. sea salt
¼ tsp. freshly ground black pepper

Work flour into egg in a bowl. Add soda water and mix roughly with a chopstick. Season with salt and pepper. The batter should be slightly lumpy, not smooth. Refrigerate until ready to use. Add extra soda water if batter looks too thick.

## CARAMELIZED ONION

Serve as a condiment, use as a tart filling, or even add to bread dough. Cook finely sliced sweet onions in a good quantity of olive oil in a wide, heavy-bottomed pan over moderate heat until onion caramelizes and tastes sweet. Strain, reserving the flavored oil for other cooking. Keeps, refrigerated in a sealed container, for up to 2 weeks.

## WHOLE ROASTED SHALLOTS

Roast shallots in a little olive oil in a wide, heavy-bottomed pan over moderate heat until soft and sweet. Strain, reserving the flavored oil for other cooking. Keeps, refrigerated, for up to 2 weeks.

## FRIED SHALLOT SLICES

Made from red Asian shallots, these crisp, wafery slices can be sprinkled over stir-fries, noodle dishes, curries, and so on for a richly flavored texture contrast. They can be bought from Asian food stores, but are easy to make at home. Slice shallots finely lengthwise and fry in a good quantity of vegetable oil over moderate heat until golden brown – the shallots should float freely in the oil as they cook. Remove pan from heat immediately and pour the hot oil through a sieve into a stainless steel bowl. Spread fried shallots on paper towels to drain and cool. Reserve flavored oil for other cooking. Store shallots in a sealed container to keep them crisp.

## FRIED GARLIC SLICES

Garlic cloves can be sliced finely and cooked and stored in the same manner as Fried Shallot Slices (see above).

## FISH STOCK

heads and bones of 2 large fish
6 scallions, chopped
1 knob ginger, sliced
1 tsp. white peppercorns
2 cups (500 ml) dry white wine
cold water

Wash fish heads thoroughly to remove all blood. Discard gills as they will make the stock bitter. Put all ingredients into a stockpot, adding cold water to cover. Bring to the boil and simmer on low heat, skimming frequently to remove any scum, for 2 hours. Strain through a conical sieve, pressing to extract as much juice as possible. Discard solids. Strain again through a fine mesh sieve

to remove all sediment. Cool and refrigerate or freeze, unless using immediately.
*Makes about 3 qt. (3 l)*

Note: Use good-quality, fresh, cleaned fish heads and bones as they will affect the flavor of the stock. Any deep-sea white-fleshed fish is suitable.

## SHRIMP STOCK

6 medium tomatoes
2 lb. (1 kg) shrimp heads and shells
½ cup (100 ml) Chinese Shaoxing rice wine
3½ tbsp. (50 ml) vegetable oil
1 medium onion, chopped
6 cloves garlic, sliced
3 slices ginger
2 slices galangal (see Note)
1 stalk lemongrass, finely sliced
2 Thai chilies, chopped
1 tsp. Sichuan peppercorns
1 tsp. fennel seeds
1 star anise
2 kaffir lime leaves, chopped
3 qt. (3 l) Fish Stock (page 201)

Preheat oven to moderately hot at 400°F (200°C) and roast whole tomatoes for 20 minutes, or until colored and softened. Heat a large wok and add shrimp heads and shells. Toss over high heat until they start to color, then add rice wine and stir, scraping to dissolve all browned bits in pan. Remove from heat. Heat oil in a stockpot and add remaining ingredients, except stock. Cook over moderate heat until mixture starts to color and become aromatic. Add cooked shrimp heads and shells and their juices, tomatoes, and stock. Bring to the boil and simmer for 2 hours, skimming frequently to remove any scum. Strain through a conical sieve, pressing to extract as much juice as possible. Discard solids. Strain again through a fine mesh sieve to remove all sediment. Cool and refrigerate or freeze, unless using immediately.
*Makes about 3 qt. (3 l)*

Note: Lobster or crab stock can be made in the same manner. If galangal is unavailable, add another 2 slices of ginger.

## WHITE CHICKEN STOCK

1 chicken carcass
1 free-range, corn-fed chicken
several slices ginger
handful of scallion tops
several white peppercorns, freshly cracked
2 cups (500 ml) dry white wine
cold water

Wash chicken carcass in cold water to remove all blood. Put all ingredients into a stockpot and add cold water to cover. Bring to the boil over low heat and simmer, skimming frequently to remove any scum, for 2 hours. Remove solids carefully (strip meat from chicken and keep for another use) and discard bones. Strain stock through a fine mesh sieve to remove all sediment. Cool and refrigerate or freeze, unless using immediately.
*Makes about 3 qt. (3 l)*

## BROWN CHICKEN STOCK

Roasting the bones and vegetables makes this stock darker and more flavorful than its more subtle white counterpart.

3 lb. (1.5 kg) chicken carcasses
½ cup (125 ml) red wine
6 medium tomatoes
vegetable oil
1 medium onion, chopped
2 medium carrots, chopped
1 head garlic, cut in half
3 scallions, chopped
1 knob ginger, sliced
1 bay leaf
½ tsp. black peppercorns
handful of flat-leaf parsley
2½ qt. (2½ l) White Chicken Stock (see above)

Preheat oven to moderately hot at 400°F (200°C). Brown chicken carcasses in a roasting pan to render some of their fat. Add wine and deglaze pan to dissolve all browned bits. While bones are browning, roast whole tomatoes in another pan for 20 minutes, or until colored and softened. Heat a little oil in a large stockpot and cook onion, carrots, garlic, scallions, and ginger until fragrant. Stir in bay leaf, peppercorns, and parsley, then add browned bones and pan juices, tomatoes, and stock. Bring to the boil and simmer, uncovered, for 3 to 4 hours, skimming frequently to remove fat and scum. Strain stock through a conical sieve, pressing firmly to extract as much juice as possible. Discard solids. Strain again through a fine mesh sieve to remove all sediment. Allow to settle and remove any fat that rises to the top. Return stock to rinsed-out pot, bring to the boil and reduce slightly for a thicker consistency and richer flavor, if required. Cool and refrigerate or freeze, unless using immediately.

*Makes about 3 qt. (3 l)*

Note: Make duck stock in a similar manner when you have used the meat for another purpose – the bones have far too much flavor to throw out after only one use.

### RED BRAISING STOCK

A master stock for red braising is a mandatory preparation in the kitchens of northern China. This stock should never be thrown out – as long as it is brought to the boil every week, and is kept refrigerated in a sealed container, it will grow better and richer with age and can be kept topped up. Every time you cook meat in it, just make sure you strain the stock through a fine mesh sieve before refrigerating (this keeps it free of particles that may cause bacteria to grow). My master stock is now eight years old and I use it constantly as I am addicted to food cooked in it.

This master stock gives a rich, reddish-brown, lacquered appearance and a wonderfully penetrating flavor and aroma to meat and poultry. As Ken Hom says in the *Encyclopedia of Chinese Cookery Techniques*, it is a stock "that is at once salty from the two types of soy sauces; sweet from the sugar; spicy on account of the peppercorns, anise, and fennel seeds; and mellow from the rice wine." As the process of red braising is a very gentle one, it also gives anything cooked in it a tender, velvety texture.

3 qt. (3 l) White Chicken Stock (page 202)
1¼ cups (300 ml) dark soy sauce
1 cup (250 ml) soy sauce

½ cup (100 ml) Chinese Shaoxing rice wine
3 tbsp. (40 g) Chinese yellow rock sugar (available from Asian/Chinese food stores)
2 star anise, broken
2 pieces cassia bark
1 tsp. fennel seeds
1 tsp. Sichuan peppercorns
1 black cardamom pod, cracked
2 pieces dried orange peel
2 Thai chilies, split lengthwise
4 slices ginger
2 slices fresh galangal (see Note)
3 pieces licorice root

Bring all ingredients to the boil in a large stockpot. Simmer on very low heat for 1 hour, then strain through a fine mesh sieve. Discard solids. Cool completely before refrigerating in a sealed container.

*Makes about 4 qt. (4 l)*

Note: If galangal is unavailable, add 2 more slices of ginger.

### BEEF/VEAL STOCK

This is a rich stock, made from roasted beef bones, shanks, and veal knuckles, that forms the basis of good sauces and soups with great depth of flavor.

2 lb. (1 kg) beef bones
2 lb. (1 kg) split shanks
2 lb. (1 kg) veal knuckles
5 medium tomatoes, halved
2 medium onions, chopped
1 large carrot, chopped
vegetable oil
2 cups (500 ml) red wine
handful of flat-leaf parsley
4 tsp. black peppercorns
2 sprigs of thyme
cold water

Preheat oven to moderately hot at 400°F (200°C) and brown bones in a roasting pan for 30 minutes. While bones are cooking, toss whole tomatoes with onion, carrot, and a little oil in another roasting pan and roast until softened. Put bones into a large stockpot – there should be room to spare. Remove any fat from baking

pan, add wine, and deglaze pan to dissolve all browned bits. Tip wine and juices into stock. Add vegetables to stockpot with remaining ingredients and cover with cold water. Bring to the boil, reduce heat, and simmer for 6 hours, skimming regularly to remove scum. Carefully remove bones and strain stock through a conical sieve. Discard solids. Strain again through a fine mesh sieve to remove all sediment. Skim off any excess fat from surface with a ladle. Cool and refrigerate or freeze, unless using immediately. If your recipe calls for reduced stock or a demi-glace, simply cook stock until its volume is reduced and it becomes thicker and more unctuous – demi-glace should coat the back of a spoon.
*Makes about 5 qt. (5 l)*

## SPICED VEGETABLE STOCK

This versatile vegetable stock can be made ahead of time. It can be used as a base for a vegetable curry, added to a stir-fry or enriched with coconut milk to make a sauce.

1 head garlic
6 dried Chinese black mushrooms
2 cups (500 ml) warm water
2 tbsp. (30 ml) vegetable oil
1 medium onion, chopped
2 carrots, peeled and finely sliced
1 stalk celery (with leaves), chopped
1 tbsp. minced ginger
5 scallions, sliced
3 Thai chilies, sliced
2 tsp. black peppercorns
2 tsp. Sichuan peppercorns
1 tbsp. minced fresh turmeric (see Note)
2 qt. (2 l) cold water
1 stalk lemongrass, finely sliced
3½ tbsp. (50 ml) fish sauce

Preheat oven to moderate at 350°F (180°C). Wrap garlic in aluminum foil and roast for 30 minutes, or until softened. Unwrap and separate the cloves. Meanwhile, soak dried mushrooms in warm water for 15 minutes, or until softened. Heat oil in a stockpot and sweat onion, carrots, celery, ginger, scallions, chili, and roasted garlic over low heat for about 15 minutes, or until softened. Add mushrooms and their soaking liquid, black and Sichuan

peppercorns, turmeric, and cold water and bring to the boil. Simmer for 30 minutes. Add lemongrass and fish sauce and simmer for a further 15 minutes. Strain through a fine mesh sieve. Discard solids. Cool and refrigerate or freeze, unless using immediately.
*Makes about 2 qt. (2 l)*

Note: If fresh turmeric is unavailable, substitute 1 tsp. ground turmeric.

## EGG NOODLES

The following quantities are sufficient for the dishes in this book that include egg noodles. However, if you want to make noodles the feature of a meal, just increase the quantities – simply multiply the ingredients as required.

3 large eggs
4 tsp. (20 ml) olive oil
1⅔ cups (250 g) bread flour
pinch of sea salt
rice flour, for dusting

Blend all ingredients, except rice flour, in a food processor until dough forms a ball. Wrap in plastic wrap and refrigerate for 1 hour. Cut dough into 4 pieces and flatten each piece by hand or with a rolling pin. Pass each piece through rollers of a pasta machine, starting on the widest setting and working your way through each setting until you reach the finest. Dust dough with rice flour each time before moving onto next setting to prevent sticking (rice flour is free of glutens, which could toughen the dough at this stage). Hang sheets of dough over a broom handle or back of a chair to dry for 10 minutes – this makes dough easier to cut. Pass through spaghetti cutters on your pasta machine, then hang noodles over a broom handle or back of a chair for 30 minutes, or until ready to cook. Bring a large saucepan of water to a rolling boil, add noodles, and allow water to return to the boil. Cook for 2 minutes, remove noodles with a sieve, and drain. If not eating immediately, refresh noodles under cold running water to stop them cooking, then drain and toss lightly with a little oil to prevent sticking. To reheat, immerse noodles in boiling water for 10 seconds, then drain.
*Serves 3 to 4 as a main course*

# INDEX